The Hidden Agenda

A Look Beyond the Emerging Church

By
Jan Voerman

Expanded Second Edition

"Before the final visitation of God's judgments upon the earth there will be among the people of the Lord such a revival of primitive godliness as has not been witnessed since apostolic times... The enemy of souls desires to hinder this work; and before the time for such a movement shall come, he will endeavor to prevent it by introducing a counterfeit. In those churches which he can bring under his deceptive power he will make it appear that God's special blessing is poured out; there will be manifest what is thought to be great religious interest. Multitudes will exult that God is working marvelously for them, when the work is that of another spirit. Under a religious guise, Satan will seek to extend his influence over the Christian world." (E. G. White, *The Great Controversy*, p. 464.)

TEACH Services, Inc.
www.TEACHServices.com

World rights reserved. This book or any portion thereof may not be copied or reproduced in any form or manner whatever, except as provided by law, without the written permission of the publisher, except by a reviewer who may quote brief passages in a review.

The author assumes full responsibility for the accuracy of all facts and quotations as cited in this book.

The opinions expressed in this book are the author's personal views and interpretation of the Bible and do not necessarily reflect those of TEACH Services, Inc.

Copyright © 2007, 2011 TEACH Services, Inc.
ISBN-13: 978-1-57258-672-7 (Paperback)
ISBN-13: 978-1-57258-978-0 (Ebook)
Library of Congress Control Number: 2011923668

Published by
TEACH Services, Inc.
www.TEACHServices.com

Table of Contents

Foreword v
Introduction vii
1. No Response 1
2. Imminent danger 3
3. Remarkable 6
4. Another Tsunami 8
5. Alpha Course 10
6. Toronto 16
7. Miracles 19
8. Joy Without Prayer 22
9. Vancouver 25
10. Urgent Question 28
11. Toronto—Alpha—Willow Creek—Saddleback 33
12. Alpha Conference 37
13. Seeker Friendly 43
14. Another Gospel 48
15. Inaccuracies 54
16. Prophecy 59
17. Immortality 64
18. Lutheran Praesidium 65
19. Willow Creek Captures SDA Pastors 68
20. A Firm Stand 74
21. Sincere Conversion 77
22. Commercial Methods 81
23. Total Quality Management 83

24. Shape	86
25. New Age	93
26. Traditional and Modern Magic	103
27. New Age Pantheism	108
28. Occultism	111
29. Freemasonry	118
30. Meditation	128
31. 'Breath Prayers'	138
32. Resisters	151
33. Critical Voices	163
34. Angels	170
35. Drums	173
36. Neutral Music?	180
37. Temple-Service	186
38. Heavenly Music	192
Appendix I — Crosslinked Influences	195
Appendix II — Toronto & Kundalini	197
Appendix III — God's Church & The Paradigm Church	200
Appendix IV — Breaking News	202

Foreword

In the present religious world, there is a temptation to look to the outside for answers. People look for peace, hoping beyond hope to find it. Today, the world looks to such things as nuclear armaments, genetic engineering, and financial security to calm their greatest fears. Those involved in church growth often succumb to the mass marketing techniques used to assure humanity that stability, peace, and prosperity are just around the corner. They often surrender spiritual development to the specialities of secular professionals rather than to ministers of the Word of God. While the field of education may reveal some insights as to methods of information transfer and politics may disclose techniques for intriguing the masses, yet such are not applicable in the halls of the sanctuary.

The Hidden Agenda portrays the contemporary Third Revival, which finds its roots in the American Pentecostal Revivalist movement, and describes how its tentacles enter main-stream churches selling hope. The so-called Third Revival movement is currently experiencing phenomenal growth, with the development of mega-churches, each playing host to tens of thousands of members, and the spawning of an entire pop culture, complete with media, literature, and lifestyle. What denomination or church group would not embrace such successful methods for recruiting new members? *The Hidden Agenda* gives serious consideration to this question. Jan Voerman's thesis is disarming in its specificity: there is a danger in rebuilding the church under the influence of secular mass-marketing techniques. *The Hidden Agenda* seeks to outline those dangers by turning the reader to the historical roots of the Third Revival and some of its most vocal advocates, the Alpha Movement, Rick Warren and The Purpose Driven Life, and others.

One concerned critic of Rick Warren comments:

As church leaders and secular leaders alike have found themselves in awe of this man's Purpose Driven paradigm, I, as a believer in Jesus Christ, have been in awe too. But my amazement isn't over Rick Warren's plans to save the world; no, my amazement is over Christian leaders and their blindness to what is really taking place. They have been overtaken and lured by a seductive spirituality that calls itself Purpose Driven, emerging church, seeker-friendly and a number of other names but has its origin in the Garden of Eden when the serpent said, 'You will be like God.' (D. Dombrowski, Commentary on "Can Rick Warren Save the World?" Fox News Title, August 17, 2006.)

The Hidden Agenda carefully analyzes the current state of church-growth methodologies in groups following the Third Revival movement. While Third Revival techniques do fill pews, often to overflowing, these same techniques fail to fill the spiritual vacuum existing in humans. The blending of New Age, Eastern mysticism, and ecumenicism with the good news of the gospel provides a poor foundation for solving the problem of spiritual emptiness. The downplaying of Scripture in favor of more user-friendly and relationship-based approach tends to turn the attention of members to self rather than God.

Jan Voerman's purpose in *The Hidden Agenda* is not only to warn the reader a false spirituality is creeping into the church, but also to point the way back to the true worship of God found in Scripture.

I heartily recommend this book and urge the reader to consider its conclusions.

—Conrad L. Demsky, Reviewer

Introduction

There is a very fascinating prophecy in the book *The Great Controversy* by Ellen White:

> Through spiritualism, Satan appears as a benefactor of the race, healing the diseases of the people, and professing to present a new and more exalted system of religious faith; but at the same time he works as a destroyer. His temptations are leading multitudes to ruin... (p. 589)

Note the words "a new and more exalted system of religious faith". That is exactly what the New Age claims to do. Its goals are to infiltrate all religions with its basic concepts. It teaches that we are all little gods and therefore immortal. It believes that all religions, including pagan, can lead to "heaven". It further believes that anyone who refuses to accept these concepts should be dealt with.

Of course these concepts strike at the very heart of biblical Christianity. The authority of Scripture would be totally undermined. While giving lip service to Jesus it would destroy the teaching of the atoning sacrifice. In this view since everyone is already a "god", the authority of the Law of God would be destroyed. Man would have the right to change and adjust the Ten Commandments to meet the needs of a modern world.

Playing on the immortal god concept, evil spirits masquerading as good spirits will find entrance into the mind of man. They will lead mankind and world leaders into horrible choices, all the while thinking that they are doing the will of God. This will result in a global melt down of civil behavior. It will bring a time of trouble such as the world has never known. Nor can we even now anticipate the horror.

These evil spirits under the disguise of good will get the worship and obedience of most of the world. When that infiltration is complete we will see the formation of Babylon the Great as predicted in

Revelation.

This infiltration of pagan concepts has long been documented in the Roman Catholic church. In more recent times it's infiltration into main line Protestant churches can be found. But the Evangelicals have long resisted this. But now these concepts are moving rapidly into Evangelicals. With these new developments Evangelicals and Rome are rushing to work together not on just religious issues but more importantly a common political agenda. The script we are watching being played is right out of Revelation 12 to 18.

Jan Voerman shows the flow of the infiltration. The research and information will be amazing. Surely we are moving toward the predictions of Revelation 13 when all the world will be astounded by these miracle working powers. Once Babylon has a hold on political power, the next step will be to persecute mercilessly those that refuse to go along.

Never was there a time when we need to test everything by Scripture! We are entering into the time when "if it were possible even the very elect would be deceived."

This is not a book to enjoy. It's message is sobering. It should force us to take stock of our own spiritual condition. Hopefully it will drive us to our knees and to the Bible and the Spirit of prophecy. It provides powerful documentation to these great movements that will influence the entire world to repeat on a global scale, the horrors of the fall of Jerusalem in A.D. 70.

—Jay Gallimore

Chapter 1

No Response

Martin Gray was a Jewish boy from the ghetto of Warsaw. The Germans had taken Poland and all the Jews were systematically evacuated to extermination camps. Martin Gray was, along with his family and many other Jews, crammed in carriages and send to Treblinka. Martin was lucky, he wasn't immediately gassed. Together with a couple of other Jewish young people he had to clean the carriages; throw the bodies out of the gas chambers into ditches and sort the clothes that were put into great sacks and loaded into the cars.

One day Martin saw the opportunity to hide between the clothes in a car and when the train drove out of the camp he succeeded, with feverish efforts, to make an opening with a pocketknife and remove a few boards of the car through which he jumped out while the train moved. Fortunately he didn't hurt himself too much as he landed in a grassy ditch. After a couple of days of wandering around he came to Zambro, where he found a Jewish community still living in freedom.

Immediately he began to warn people about the coming danger. Martin told them about the terror of Treblinka—about the gruesome things he had been through. But the people only looked at him with astonishment and they didn't take him seriously. How hard he tried and urged the people: You have to flee; soon it will be your turn; you still can go now... it all didn't help. The people of his own race declared him to be insane and said to him: Impossible! The Germans aren't that stupid. Why would they want to kill us? As long as we pay and work for them nothing will happen to us. The Germans need us. It is for their own good that we will stay alive.

But Martin knew better. He tried to make them realize the reality.

However a short and corpulent man with a smooth talk said, "Don't listen to him, he must be insane!" His words kept the people away from Martin and they made fun of him and laughed.

Martin did everything he could, but despite his serious and earnest warnings, no one responded. Martin wrote in his book:

> What a nightmare to know, to be sure that you're right and not to be able to convince people...I was a sort of tragic clown...In the morning, at dawn, I was outside the synagogue, preaching tirelessly, buttonholing passersby and trying to convince them, but as the days went by my words lost even their original impact. (Martin Gray, *For Those I Loved*, Little, Brown and Company, Boston, Toronto, 1971, p. 166.)

Tragic...very tragic! Not long afterwards Zambro was surrounded by the Germans and all the Jews were rounded up to face their doom.

The question for us today remains: *Are we open to investigate critical information and verify the facts?*

When we are dealing with systems of belief and forms of worship we even move beyond our present being into eternal realities. How much more significant the consequences are!

Chapter 2

Imminent danger

With regard to this late moment of earth's history, God's holy Word has many warnings applicable to us. Some people, however, seem to prefer not to read these passages, because what the Bible says does not support the euphoria with which they surround themselves. Nevertheless, Paul writes: "This know also, that in the last days perilous times shall come." (2 Tim. 3:1.) And the apostle Peter says: "Knowing this first, that there shall come in the last days scoffers, walking after their own lusts." (2 Pet. 3:3.)

Jesus Himself gave warning in His speech about the last things: "Take heed that no man deceive you...many false prophets shall rise, and shall deceive many." (Matt. 24:4, 11.)

We are also informed: "they will not endure sound doctrine; but after their own lusts, shall they heap to themselves teachers, having itching ears; And they shall turn away their ears from the truth, and shall be turned unto fables." (2 Tim. 4:3, 4.)

We certainly live in stirring times in which we should be very watchful. But the remarkable thing is that when some have the courage to warn of the imminent dangers that are surrounding us, many will look at them with surprise. Some make fun, laugh, or call them prophets of doom. "Oh no!" they will say, "We do not need to worry. It will be: 'peace, peace, and no danger'. We are entering a new future. A new world-order is coming on soon with a unified religion of love and brotherhood".

However, the Bible paints a more gloomy picture of the time of the End when Biblical truth is no longer of paramount importance. Many will prefer to listen to nice fairy tales and fables. The book of

Revelation even speaks about the whole earth that is wondering after the beast that speaks blasphemy.

Yes, all that dwell upon the earth shall worship the beast and the dragon! If you doubt this and if you don't realize what that means, read then Revelation 13:3, 4, 8 which clearly says that all the world wondered after the beast...and they worshipped the dragon...and the beast. The previous chapter tells us that the dragon is the old serpent, called the Devil and Satan, who deceives the whole earth. (Rev. 12:9.)

Nobody needs to remain ignorant concerning the dangers that threaten everyone on earth in the time of the End. We should not underestimate our situation. Will man heed the warning voice? But how will it be possible that all who dwell on the earth shall wonder after the beast?

How can the whole earth in this modern and enlightened time be so deceived that they will worship Satan? Isn't that unimaginable? We are not living in the dark middle ages, are we? There is so much knowledge and wisdom in so many different areas, how can everybody then be so deceived? Could it possibly be that the Bible has not given us reliable information?

As we look at the Christian churches what we see is a revival taking place! How then can the book of Revelation call the end time churches heathen, Babylon and describe it as a dwelling place of devils and unclean spirits? Well-considered courses and seminars about church-growth, and how to live as a good Christian are held in many countries. This appears to be most successful as we see large congregations arise—mega churches—with thousands of members who claim to come together in the spirit of Christ to praise and worship God. Praise-services are organized everywhere to honour and worship God with all sorts of songs and musical instruments. Churches appear to revive with these new kinds of worship. How then can the Bible picture the whole world backsliding religiously so that they will worship the dragon?

Furthermore, Alpha courses are offered on all continents and with the help of the Willow Creek and Saddleback models, new purpose-driven congregations are formed everywhere to bring unbelievers and addicted men and women into the church and to preach to them the message of salvation. Isn't that a wonderful and praiseworthy development? And if you think these activities could be ignored, consider then that the handbook, *Purpose Driven Church*, by Rick Warren, preacher of the Saddleback church, was translated into 21 languages by 2003, and that, by now, its principles are applied by thousands and thousands of churches everywhere around the world.

In the year 2000 there were 18,000 Churches in 122 countries that studied the Alpha course, while the materials were available in 33 languages. This isn't a small thing and it continues to grow. Almost 29,000 Alpha courses were offered with more than six million participants in many different churches in the year 2004. In England the course was given in more than 7,000 churches and universities in 2004. A newspaper reported that almost everybody on the streets of London has heard about the Alpha course. More than 1500 advertising signs; 3,000 buses and many taxi-cabs advertised in October 2004 about the Alpha course and hundreds of thousands leaflets, posters and brochures were printed to get the residents of England acquainted with Alpha.

On the religious level it is one of the best known initiatives of this time to which most churches and religious groups have opened their doors.

But despite the fact that the course seems to be accepted worldwide and important character principles are advocated, we need to realize that Satan's strategy is to mix good with evil. Therefore we should always test what is truth. To prove all things and hold fast that which is good has always been beneficial under all circumstances. When the majority accepts something as true is no guarantee that it really is truth and reliable.

We should ask ourselves, what is the driving force behind the church-growth movement? And though some aspects of its methods appear useful, we should, nevertheless, carefully consider the possible results and consequences.

Chapter 3

Remarkable

Most Christians believe it is praiseworthy to follow the example of the believers at Berea, who distinguished themselves by daily searching the Scriptures to find out if the things that were told them were true. (Acts 17:11) It is remarkable, however, that so few follow this example with regard to matters that are widely accepted and seem to be successful.

The editor of the African magazine *Sentinel* writes:

> But what really hurts is when a deceived person is shown the facts and you get one of two reactions. Either the person refuses to look at the facts, or he looks at it with the attitude of, "don't confuse me with the facts, I've already made up my mind." *(Rick Warren & Saddleback Church,* Kies, P.O. Box 8009, Edleen 1625, Africa.)

Nevertheless, we as Christians are called to follow the Biblical way by not only taking heed of ourselves, but also of the doctrine, and we are called to persevere. Says the apostle, "for in doing this thou shalt both save thyself, and them that hear thee." (1 Tim. 4:16)

Therefore it is a life and death matter that we stand up for the things that match with sound doctrine. (Titus 2:1) We also read:

"Whosoever...abideth not in the doctrine of Christ, hath not God." That's very clear language! No matter how beautiful and pious someone's words might be, the Bible clearly tells us that he who doesn't adhere to the doctrine of Christ doesn't have God on his side. God will not be with him, even if he is applying wonderful principles and has great success and is very diligent; it will not benefit him. God will finally answer: "I never knew you." (see Matt. 7:21–23) The passage confirms: "He that abideth in the doctrine of Christ, he hath both the

Father and the Son." (2 John 9)

If we want to know if something is from God, we should not be guided by whether it appeals and appears successful or not. Neither should we follow nice sounding words, impressive spectacles, or pleasant feelings.

No, the doctrine of Christ, God's holy Word, should be the standard, and everything that we can bring in harmony with that, can be accepted, applied, and proclaimed as true and reliable.

Chapter 4

Another Tsunami

Sunday morning, the 26th of December 2004, a huge catastrophic tidal wave destroyed great parts of several South-Asian countries around the Indian Ocean. More than 250,000 people lost their lives because of this sudden natural disaster. Before the tsunami came about, the sea withdrew and large areas of the beach became dry. Thousands of people didn't know to discern this ominous sign and walked unsuspectingly around on the beach, fascinated by the interesting things they saw there. Here and there was a floundering fish that hadn't been in pace with the rapid backwashing water, and the attention of many people was distracted from the imminent danger. And so they didn't realize the gravity of the situation. Thus the quickly following ill-fated event claimed many thousands of unfortunate victims.

But there is another tsunami; another gigantic wave that rolls across the country that doesn't claim thousands, but millions of unsuspecting victims. And the unhappy thing is that most people don't realize it. Indeed, they are often unwilling to be warned. They are fascinated by the interesting things that are presented and they don't discern the sinister omens.

C. Peter Wagner, professor of church growth at Fuller Theological Seminary School of World Mission wrote several books on church growth and is a leading proponent of Third Wave methodology. He identifies the first Wave as the Pentecostal movement, the second, the charismatic movement; while the third wave, the signs and wonders movement, is now joining them.

Concerning this, John F. MacArthur, Jr., warns:

> Unsuspecting churches and denominations have opened their doors—and their pulpits—to Third Wave teachers, many of whom sport very impressive academic credentials. **The Third Wave is now rolling like a destructive tsunami, leaving chaos and confusion in its wake.** (*Charismatic Chaos*, (Pocket) Zondervan, 1992, p. 158, emphasis added.)

Here we have a tsunami that claims millions of victims. This tsunami is the "Third Wave of Signs and Wonders"!

MacArthur goes on to say,

> Third Wave devotees believe that fantastic signs and wonders demonstrate the genuineness of their movement. Miraculous phenomena are the very heart of the Third Wave credo. Third Wavers are persuaded that miracles, visions, tongues, prophecies, and healings are essential supplements to the gospel. They view Christianity without those things as impotent, adulterated by the Western, materialistic mindset.
>
> Signs and wonders are the key to Third Wave evangelism. Some Third Wavers even say that unbelievers must experience the miraculous to be brought to full faith. Merely preaching the gospel message, they believe, will never reach the world for Christ. Most people will not believe without seeing miracles, they say, and those who do will be inadequately converted and therefore stunted in their spiritual growth. (Ibid., pp. 158, 159.)

Thus millions of people around the world are distracted by exciting things—the necessary miraculous, in order to be brought to full faith. This draws their attention from the pure and powerful two-edged sword of the gospel message that is thus itself regarded as invalid to reach the world for Christ and bring about true and full conversion.

The Toronto movement, particularly, is attended with miraculous phenomena of signs and wonders. But the Alpha Course, Willow Creek, Saddleback, and other mega churches, are also clearly infecting millions who are misled and pulled along by them.

Chapter 5

Alpha Course

The Alpha course was developed at the Anglican HTB Church (Holy Trinity Brompton) in London in the 1980s. Nicky Gumbel, pastor of this church, developed the course to its present form which is generally dealt with in 10 to 12 weeks.

Each program starts with a meal. After that there is an introduction about the subject, followed by a discussion in small groups. **An important part of the course is a weekend about the Holy Spirit with a special evening for miraculous healing and fulfillment of the Holy Spirit.** The end of the course is celebrated along with invited friends who are being encouraged to participate in the next course.

The course isn't confronting, but reckons with personal conviction and cultural circumstances and tries to break down barriers. It emphasizes only that which all the churches have in common. The plan is to facilitate a relaxed atmosphere with a unified spirit in which participants feel at home.

The most significant factor in this pattern of psychological manipulation is the recommendation to lay the Bible aside, so no one will be deterred. It is also customary not to say a prayer at the end of the meeting, since some guests might be embarrassed. Indeed, the manual itself states: "During the meal speaking about God and faith is taboo." (*NL* edition, p. 13.)

To rightly judge the author and the course it is important to know some background-information about the London Brompton church and Nicky Gumbel.

John Wimber spoke in 1982 at the Brompton church and by his prayer Nicky Gumbel received the power of the Spirit. Nicky himself tells us about this experience:

> After he had been praying for about 30 seconds, all I can say is I felt this incredible power—it was like 10.000 volts...going through my body. In fact, it was so powerful that after a bit I couldn't take it any more but I think he had only just got onto the ministry team because he only had one prayer and it was 'More power, Lord!' And every time he prayed this prayer, the power increased! So after a bit I couldn't take it any longer and I started praying against him! I started saying, 'No more power, Lord!' But he carried on praying, 'More power, Lord!' So eventually there was this shouting match going on in the middle of the room. John Wimber...said, 'Take that one out!' So they carried me out through the French windows! And as I was being carried out John Wimber said, 'God is giving to that man power to tell people about Jesus Christ.' And I have often looked back at that as a very significant moment in my life. (*Talk 13*, HTB 2000.)

It was after this that Nicky Gumbel developed the Alpha course. But who is John Wimber actually? Wimber got his knowledge from occult, New Age sources. He stood enthusiastically behind Mary Baker Eddy, the founder of Christian Science. He declares that God Himself, back in 1977, gave him the assignment to preach forgiveness of sins and to apply physical healing.

Wimber exerted himself toward union with the Catholic Church. He was filled with praise for the pope and the Catholic Church and at a conference in Anaheim, where about 5,000 pastors were united, he offered to the present Catholic archbishop, on behalf of the Protestant Church, his apology for the fact that the Protestant Church left the Catholic Church and for everything that was said about his church. (Dave Hunt, *Occult Invasion*, pp. 121, 204, 502, 536, 568, 597.)

Significantly, E. G. White wrote:

> Instead of standing in defense of the faith once delivered to the saints, they are now, as it were, apologizing to Rome for their uncharitable opinion of her, begging pardon for their bigotry. (*The Great Controversy*, p. 572.)

Wimber also was leader and father of the third wave of the Holy Spirit, the Signs and Wonders movement, in which he played a crucial part. This wave is characterized by a passionate search for ecstatic experiences; for mystic phenomena, mysterious powers, and supernatural miracles; while personal prayer, Bible study, and dedicated obedience are studiously neglected. **The entire emphasis is on signs and wonders; while truth seems not to exist anymore, since every religion seems to be right.** Wimber felt as much at home with the Catholic faith as he did with the Evangelical faith and he even defended healing by relics.

John F. MacArthur reports total confusion at Wimber's Vineyard church in Anaheim:

> Wimber tried to get everyone speaking in tongues at once. Women were convulsing on the floor; one man lay on his back in a catatonic state; and all around, hundreds of people were dancing, running, shouting, and standing on chairs. (*Charismatic Chaos*, p. 158.)

Significantly, it was from this man, John Wimber, the leader of the third wave, that Nicky Gumbel received the "power of the spirit."

Another aspect of Alpha is that Gumbel and his church were touched by the "Toronto Blessing", an occult happening introduced by Ellie Mumfort. Gumbel summarizes on tape how that came about:

> We went to their house...where a group of leaders of their church was meeting...Ellie Mumford told us a little bit of what she had seen in Toronto...it was obvious that Ellie was just dying to pray for all of us...then she said, 'Now we'll invite the Holy Spirit to come,' and the moment she said that, one of the people was thrown, literally, across the room and was lying on the floor, just howling and laughing... making the most incredible noise...I experienced the power of the Spirit in a way I hadn't experienced for years, like massive electricity going through my body...One of the guys was prophesying. He was just lying there prophesying...[Gumbel returns to HTB, closes the meeting there in prayer]...I prayed "Lord, thank you so much for all you are doing and we pray you'll send your Spirit" and I was just about to say "in Jesus' name, Amen" and go out the door when the Spirit came on the people who were in the room. One of them started laughing like a hyena. (Video III, lesson 9, cited in *Alpha: New life or New Lifestyle?* p. 4.)

It isn't unusual for people to be unable to go home by themselves, after the services at the Brompton church. We read:

The Holy Trinity Brompton church always hires a taxi firm, of which the drivers know that the members of the church aren't really drunk, as it seems, and that they won't be any trouble in the taxi. (Dave Roberts, *An ihren Früchten werdet ihr sie kennen,* 1995, s. 27.)

Toronto phenomena play a significant role in Alpha's background. The Holy Spirit weekends are an important part of the Alpha Course and Gumbel says that the purpose of these weekends is to expect all kinds of strange manifestations and bodily agitations. But as we will see, there is a close relation with Eastern Kundalini Yoga.

We read:

Sometimes, when people are filled, they shake like a leaf in the wind. Others find themselves breathing deeply as if almost physically breathing in the Spirit...Physical heat sometimes accompanies the filling of the Spirit and people experience it in their hands or some other part of their bodies. One person described a feeling of "glowing all over". Another said she experienced "liquid heat". Still another described "burning in my arms when I was not hot". (*The Christian Research Network Journal,* Spring 1998, p. 21.)

We see "Toronto" symptoms such as: falling backwards, being "drunk", trembling, convulsing, and laughing. (*Alpha,* p. 42, 130f, 147.) It is, as Nicky says, no coincidence that the "Toronto movement" comes together with the rise of the Alpha course: "I think that the two of them can go well together." (*Renewal,* May, 1995, p. 15, cited in *Alpha: New Life or New Lifestyle?* p. 5.) **This admittance by Gumbel is very significant as it indicates a close relation between the Alpha course and the Toronto movement.**

The Alpha course was presented the same way for several years at the Brompton church "but it wasn't until it was connected with the 'Toronto blessing' that Alpha received international reputation." (Patrick Tschui, *Der Alpha-Kurs*...CH-8340, Hinwil, 2003, s. 7.)

But how should we view the "Toronto blessing" in relation to the Alpha course? Is it an innocent side effect or is it something to watch out for? Pastors, clergymen, and gospel workers accepted the "Toronto blessing" as a welcome revival and it has evolved worldwide.

But is the Toronto phenomenon really a blessing?

Four years before Toronto went international, Pope John Paul II predicted: "**a new injection** of life for the Church in **the next few years** would come from **the East**." It is a striking fact that Alpha and Toronto reveal manifestations that "are the same as those seen in the Eastern mystic practice of Kundalini yoga. (Elizabeth McDonald and Dusty Peterson, *Alpha, The Unofficial Guide*, Cambridge, 2004, pp. 147, 148. Emphasis present.)

Indeed, a New Age quote clearly affirms that in the Toronto movement Kundalini energy is manifested:

> The 1970s fall short when compared to the ten thousands of people who came into contact with the Kundalini **energy** since 1994 **in the so-called Toronto Blessing**... (Ibid., Emphasis present.)

Not only are the same methods of this transfer of "Kundalini energy" applied in the Toronto happening but Nicky Gumbel of the Alpha course "uses the term 'an **energy** within' to describe his Holy Spirit!" (Ibid.)

No wonder Eastern Kundalini advocates recognize their manifestations at Toronto and Alpha.

Greg DesVoignes, lists **49 similarities** between Kundalini and Toronto. (*Holy Laughter & Company, A Toronto Blessing... Or Kundalini Curse?* (Christian Research Ministries, Spokane, WA 99208.) See Appendix II.

Howard writes about the amalgamation of Toronto and Alpha:

> The Alpha Course is not really new, it was used for 16 years at Holy Trinity Brompton, yet it was unknown. What happened to make it the giant monstrosity it is today? Eleanor Mumford of the South-West London Vineyard church went to Toronto Airport Vineyard church in Canada and came back filled with the demonic manifestations of the Toronto so-called blessing, in reality a curse! Nicky Gumbel, the main instigator of Alpha, was infected with T(oronto) B(lessing), **and so the roll of Alpha began, under the empowering of the false revival and the Satanic manifestations.** (*The Alpha Course, Friend or Foe?* pp. 14, 15. Emphasis added.)

Richard Ostling wrote in 1994 that the Anglican churches in England have more resemblances with rock concerts and rugby matches than with Christian worship:

> Curate Nickey Gumbel prays that the Holy Spirit will come upon the congregation. Soon, a woman begins laughing. Others gradually join her with hearty belly laughs. A young worshipper falls to the floor, hands twitching. Another falls, then another and another. Within half an hour there are bodies everywhere as supplicants sob, shake, roar like lions, and strangest of all, laugh uncontrollably. ("Laughing for the Lord", *Time* Magazine, Aug. 15, 1994, p. 38.)

Another article from 1995 reported that people in churches worldwide are jerking spasmodically, dancing ecstatically, and acting like animals. The article reported that this behavior by Christians has already spread from Canada to roughly 7,000 congregations in Hong Kong, Norway, South Africa, and Australia, plus scores of churches in the United States. (Kenneth L. Woodward, Jeanne Gordon, Carol Hall, Barry Brown, "The Giggles Are for God," *Newsweek*, 20 Febr. 1995, p. 54.)

Chapter 6

Toronto

Rodney Howard-Browne is the key person of the Toronto movement: "the current popularity of the phenomenon can be traced to one man, Rodney Howard-Browne, formerly a Pentecostal South African evangelist." (*Holy Laughter, Rodney Howard-Browne and the Toronto Blessing,* Biblical Discernment Ministries, March 1996, p. 1.)

Rodney calls himself the "Holy Ghost Bartender," who invites everyone to taste of the new wine which he serves. He brought the revival to various countries and passed the ointment on to Randy Clark, Claudio Freidzon, Benny Hinn, and others. John Arnott, preacher of the Toronto Airport Vineyard Church, received the power of the spirit from Claudio Freidson, and from Toronto, the spiritual revival received great fame worldwide as the "Toronto Blessing."

But can we consider Rodney Howard-Browne, the leading man behind the Toronto movement, a sincere believing and dedicated Christian?

The offending and arrogant attitude that Rodney revealed towards God is quite remarkable. He himself shamelessly tells us that he at a young age set the Almighty God an ultimatum. While praying for hours he challenged God: "Either You come down here and touch me or I am going to come up there and touch You." (Rodney Howard-Browne, *Fresh Oil from Heaven,* Louisville, 1992, p. 28.)

He began shouting without ceasing: "God I want your power." (Rodney Howard-Browne, *Flowing in the Holy Ghost,* Louisville, 1991, p. 15.)

He shouted this for about 20 minutes until his voice became hoarse and those present became frightened. Rodney tells that suddenly the fire of God came upon him:

> It started on my head and went right down to my feet. His power burned in my body and stayed like that for four days. I thought I was going to die. I thought He was going to kill me… My whole body was on fire from the top of my head to the soles of my feet and out of my belly began to flow a river of living water. I began to laugh uncontrollably and then I began to weep and then speak with other tongues…I was so intoxicated on the wine of the Holy Ghost that I was beside myself. The fire of God was coursing through my whole being and it didn't quit…Because of this encounter with the Lord, my life was radically changed from that day on. (Howard Browne, *Fresh Oil from Heaven*, p. 27, 28.)

Rodney's demand that God give him this experience reminds us of the Bible-verse: "Be not deceived; God is not mocked: for whatsoever a man soweth, that shall he also reap." (Gal. 6:7)

Are good fruits reaped? The different unordered and noisy manifestations of the Toronto movement are: unrestrained laughing, uncontrolled making of animal sounds, and all kinds of disorderly behaviour and unintentional body-movements, while the Bible specifically says that self-control is the fruit of the Spirit, while everything has to be done in a decent and orderly fashion. (Gal. 5:23, NEB. 1 Cor. 14:40)

Rodney also tells about the time he spoke at the Oral Roberts University about Hell. The listeners were touched and started laughing and the more he spoke about Hell the more they laughed. But what is there so funny about Hell? At another time there was uncontrolled laughing during the dedication prayer of the Lords supper, one of the most solemn parts of the church services. (Stephen Sizer, *R. Howard-Browne, A Critical Examination of his Theology and Practice,* Christian News & Views: Newsletter & Resource Page, p. 4.)

If one is filled and moved by the Holy Spirit, how can such disturbing and dishonourable phenomena take place during such a sacred service? And what about the animal sounds?

> One who is convicted of sin might well laugh or cry *after* he has felt release from the condemnation and control of sin, which comes with confession and repentance. But there is no evidence he will bark like a dog or make other animal noises. The manifestations have historically been attributed to demonic spirits, not to the Holy

Spirit...Are we to assume that those who bark like dogs are heralding the triumph of Christ in some other form? Dogs are unclean animals (as are lions). Can we imagine Jesus or any of the apostles barking like dogs or roaring like lions? Yet who was more filled with the Holy Spirit than they? (*Holy Laughter, Rodney Howard-Browne and the Toronto Blessing,* Biblical Discernment Ministries, March 1996. p. 4.)

Chapter 7

Miracles

The healing of Sarah Lilliman, has been publicized as one of the most outstanding of the Toronto miracles. Sarah was blind, paralyzed, and mentally disturbed and a friend got a message: "Jesus said: 'Go Pray for Sarah, your friend, I'm going to heal her.'" After two hours of imploring prayer Sarah was healed and much attention was given to this incident as a proof of God's power being active in the Toronto movement. But the awkward thing about this "sensational miracle" is that Sarah and her family still have to contend with her physical problems and psychosomatic disorders, just as before. The truth simply is that there was no real healing.

Kristy is another story. Her pastor was filled with doubt when he went to Toronto but he returned as a believer. He was convinced that the power he had experienced there was real and he told his church members that he would pray for them. And the miraculous thing happened! They also received the power, but Kristy didn't, although she was longing for a deeper experience with God. She became frustrated. If this is really from God, as my pastor says it is, why is God passing me? She sat on the church floor and started crying while all around her people were touched by the spirit and were shaking, trembling, and laughing in an uncontrollable manner. When suddenly she realized that she was lying flat on the floor and that she couldn't move, her frustration gave way to fear.

When she was at last able to get up, she felt like she had just run a marathon. But instead of this experience being a powerful encouragement for a better spiritual life, as she had imagined, she began to doubt more and more as her relationship with God worsened. She didn't dare to pray or go to church and definitely did not consider the Toronto experience a blessing. She became so depressed that she had to go to the doctor for treatment. As it slowly dawned on her that it wasn't God but some other power that was active, she became convinced that these manifestations formed a rich soil for satanic deception.

She tells:

> I know there are so many believers like me who don't know. It was so gradual. When the leadership you've trusted, the leadership that seemed to be so grounded in the Word endorses this stuff, you feel guilty going against it... My story has to help others...otherwise it is a waste. I can speak from both sides now. I experienced the numbness in my body, but now I know it wasn't from God. If I can help someone, then it will be worth all the pain. I know the experience was real; now I also know how it was produced. Now more than ever, I know it wasn't from God. (Hank Hanegraaff, Christian Research Inst., CA, *Counterfeit Revival*, Word publishing, Dallas Texas, 1997, pp. 59-64.)

This is not an isolated event. Others have gone through similar experiences. It is also reported that sometimes services can get so much out of control that they end up in disorderly and immoral scenes. Women started dancing topless in a church in Sheffield at the nine o'clock service. It was on television, on the news. Over 20 women were sexually abused at the London Healing Mission: the so called "internal anointing" and we read the comment: "I don't know if the preacher wanted to be an obstetrician or a preacher." Guess what happened after this "spiritual anointing." The preacher was arrested.

At another place, women in the church service removed their knickers and Holy Communion wine was poured out over the lower part of their bodies. There are also videotapes of services where people, under the influence of the spirit, tore their clothes off their bodies and behaved immorally on the church floor. Another tendency is to "vomit in the spirit," an appearance seen during demonic manifestations. But all these crazy and disorderly scenes are by many, attributed to the working of the Spirit of God. We cannot find, however, any such immoral, inappropriate, and offensive behaviour in the Bible, as being the fruit of the Spirit.

The bewitching power appealing to the natural and sensual human being, by which the masses, who long for feelings and entertainment, are being deceived, is so strong that they cannot be convinced of the truth. Someone wrote:

> I know that what I saw in Toronto was not Biblical, but microwave ovens and toasters are not in the Bible either. They are not wrong, so why should this Toronto phenomena be wrong? (J. J. Prasch, *Why Three Years of Toronto and Still No Revival?* Moriel Ministries, pp. 5, 8.)

Chapter 8

Joy Without Prayer

John Arnott, pastor of the Toronto church, made clear: "Toronto is like a flowing stream. Don't try to test it or discern it. Just jump in, you'll understand it after you've jumped in." (J. J. Prasch, *Why Three Years of Toronto and Still No Revival?* Moriel Ministries, p. 9.)

Rodney Howard-Browne, so closely connected with the Toronto movement, says: "Don't pray. Just accept. Just receive." (Ibid.)

Also people who wait in long rows to be touched are being warned: "Wait until I come to you to lay may hands on you, but do not pray, please, do not pray." (Hank Hanegraaff, *Counterfeit Revival,* Word Publ., Dallas Texas, 1997, p. 223.)

Those who are inclined to pray, are called "stubborn." Rodney declared: "People come trying to be all serious and praying. No! This is not the time to pray. This is not a prayer meeting; get in the joy; you can pray on the way home." (Ibid.)

Counterfeit Revival leaders aim at a passive, irrational acceptance of the Spirit in much the same way as is practiced in Eastern religions.

> Like Howard-Browne and leaders of the Counterfeit Revival, the late Indian guru Baghwan Shree Rajneesh denigrates the mind, going so far as to say that the 'goal is to create a new man, one who is happily mindless...' What Hindu gurus like Baghwan Shree Rajneesh characterize as a trance state, Holy Ghost bartenders like Rodney Howard-Browne characterize as being 'drunk in the Spirit.' (Ibid. p. 225.)

This kind of apathetic acting at crucial moments in a state of dependent, passive acceptance is found in Hinduism and Buddhism but not in sincere Christianity, for God's Word clearly tells us: "Try the spirits" and "continue in prayer." (1 John 4:1; Col. 4:2) We read that the Holy Spirit is actually given to them "that ask Him." (Luke 11:13) But the Toronto leaders proclaim: "Don't pray; accept it and don't test it." (Stephen Sizer, *Rodney Howard-Browne, A Critical Examination of his Theology and Practice*, p. 4.)

Rodney says: "You can't understand what God is doing in these meetings with an analytical mind. The only way you're going to understand what God is doing is with your heart." (Ibid.)

But can we safely trust our heart? The Bible cautions: "The heart is deceitful above all things, and desperately wicked: who can know it?" (Jer. 17:9)

Another dramatic statement is: "Words have become meaningless in our society, signs and wonders are what must capture our attention." (Stephen Sizer, Ibid.)

But does this not make the proclamation of the word inferior to signs and wonders? Miraculous manifestations are to be regarded as more important and should get all the attention! Consider, however, the words that Jesus once spoke: "An evil and adulterous generation seeketh after a sign; and there shall no sign be given to it..." (Matt. 12:39)

When words prove to be powerless and meaningless, will people then, to their own benefit, adhere to signs and wonders? We read:

> If they hear not Moses and the prophets, neither will they be persuaded, though one rose from the dead. (Luke 16:31)

Signs, miracles and wonders can never take the place of inspired words.

In the time of the end, prior to the coming of the Lord, there will be a "working of Satan with all power and signs and lying wonders... in them that perish; because they received not the love of the truth, that they might be saved." (2 Thess. 2:9, 10)

These words warn us of those who consider the words of truth as words without meaning, while they occupy their minds with signs and wonders. They have heaped to themselves teachers who have turned their ears away from the truth.

And those with itching ears often show active **intolerance** towards the truth. As clearly seen throughout history, this has often led to **persecution**. Those who avert from the truth often reveal a dominant and intolerant spirit towards those that remain faithful to the truth. Concerning this Stephen Sizer justly notices: "Meanwhile, the tolerance for sound doctrine is dangerously low." (Ibid., p. 8.)

Tape recordings of Rodney's services have, especially in England, led to serious criticism. Various skilled people have recognized different kinds of phenomena in Rodney's services that are identical to voodoo practices as used by African medicine-men to evoke demons. (Clifford Hill, *PMW Team Ministries Newsletter*, 28 Nov. 1994.)

Danny Aquirre and Warren Smith make similar comparisons related to Ramakrishna, Bhagwan Rajnees, the African Kung Bushmen of the Kalahari, and with Qigong, old Chinese practices. The Indian guru Bhagwan Rajnees, for example, was known among his followers as the "divine drunkard" because he had drunk so deep from the "divine source." Many followers went to India to drink from Bhagwan's wine and when they were touched by the guru, or were near his presence, they experienced feelings of great happiness and joy. Uncontrolled laughing is also common after receiving the *Shaktipat*, the physical touch of the guru. (*Spiritual Counterfeits Project Journal, SCP Newsletter*, Fall 1994, Vol. 19, pp. 13, 14.)

Dr. Gaius Davies, psychiatrist at the King's College Hospital in London, calls the Toronto blessing a manipulation. Those present at the service are summoned many times to set aside all critical thoughts and present themselves unconditionally for the bestowment of the "blessing". The leaders are, according to Davies, bad persons, because, they misuse their power. Dr. Davies says:

> There is no sign or care or concern for the people... At HTB [Gumbel's Alpha Church, Holy Trinity Brompton] I saw individuals with a "pill rolling" action of their hands and others with serious psychological problems. These people were not being helped... They had come with real needs, but were just being manipulated. (*Reformation Today*, March/April 1995, p. 13–15.)

Chapter 9

Vancouver

Yves Brault not only visited different sensational revival services, but, at first, played also an active part in it. He writes:

> In this day and age as frantic spiritual manifestations attract the masses, becoming wilder as present-day religious leaders continually offer greater spiritual and physical benefits to their flock, an ever-increasing disregard for biblical principles and doctrines pervades the Church while many call these days the greatest revival we have ever known...I have witnessed the use of numerous manipulative and deceptive methods by popular religious leaders. This was unexpected and motivated me to examine, search and compare their teachings and methods with an in-depth study of the Scriptures. (Yves Brault, *The Intoxicating Spell of Rodney Howard-Browne, An Eye-Witness Report on the Canadian Escapades of the "Holy Ghost Bar-Tender"* 1997, Personal Freedom Outreach, P.O. Box 26062, Saint Louis, Missouri 64136, pp. 1, 2.)

This eyewitness also gave a description of the escapades of Rodney Howard-Browne, the main leader of the "laughing phenomenon" that reveals itself especially in the Toronto movement. He first visited Rodney's services at Orlando in 1992, at the church of Benny Hinn and then afterwards meetings at Vancouver in 1996, of which he gives us a description. A few remarks will give us an impression of Rodney's performance.

It was not allowed to take pictures or put the service on record and also a warning was given not to step on those that were lying on the floor, for although they were under the power of "the spirit" they still could feel pain. Interestingly, the music played a stirring part to "cheer up the crowd". This part of the service was active and inviting and lasted for about 60 to 90 minutes. We read:

> At the song, 'I Walk by Faith,' the leader urged the audience to walk sideways in the pews, which had everybody marching left and right. In a case like this, you must cooperate unless you want to be stepped on by your neighbors. The favorite 'Makes You Want to Dance,' produced delirious dancing in the crowd, where some individuals ran up front, jumping and twisting after the very first verse. (Ibid., p. 3.)

Rodney himself proves to be intolerant. He thinks it necessary to instruct the people how to laugh and behave and he focuses on those who do not react according to his wishes. It is threatening to notice how he treats the more serious people, who do not act enthusiastically: "We'll cast the religious devil out of you." (Ibid.)

There is hardly any freedom in his services. You feel intimidated and obliged to obey and agree, if you don't wish to be among Rodney's offensive category. He did not miss an opportunity in his services to embarrass his critics; those who doubt his way of acting:

> Some people have got more faith in believing the devil can come into this place tonight to touch people. How dumb can you get and still breathe! And referring to North American theologians, which he names dead heads, "Bunch of whitewash, full of dead bones, like a constipated mule." (Ibid., pp. 3, 4.)

Yves Brault reported that Rodney also played the game of faith healing. He prayed for a cancer patient and layed his hands on a woman and told about healings in previous campaigns and of course he spoke about the healing that God desires to give everybody and will confirm with signs and wonders. While he said this, he stood next to a person who translated his message into sign language for deaf people. Strangely enough Rodney didn't pray for them and he didn't lay his hands on them either. A disabled person was also neglected, as well as a young woman who was mentally disturbed. How many will have realized this?

> Howard-Browne, like faith healers, is clever, selective, and deceptive. Implying that he has an anointing from God, he threatened once again his critics or would-be critics, "If you can't produce the

real of that which you criticize you'd better shut your mouth. Just shut your mouth. Amen." (Ibid., p. 4.)

On the last day Rodney would lay his hands on everybody. After speaking for about 25 minutes he turned on a tape of a previous campaign. The technician increased the volume and a deafening applause with shouts was heard. Those present silently listened to it whereupon the volume was turned still louder. Rodney started clapping and screaming, "Jesus, Jesus." Then the crowd also began clapping and shouting and soon the men and women started dancing as if they were hypnotized. Rodney now had the crowd where he wanted them to be. "They were under his mesmeric spell." (Ibid.)

Yves Brault concludes:

> I find no edification in such meetings. Music is used as a tool to bring individuals into a hyper-suggestible emotional state, fanciful and exaggerated stories are told to gain the people's trust and confidence, and the Scriptures are misused or distorted to support their unbiblical teachings and practices. Rodney Howard-Browne not only orchestrated the show by instructing people on how to behave, but he clearly showed his arrogant nature through his statements and attitude. Where is the fear of God today? (Ibid.)

Chapter 10

Urgent Question

Yves Brault, who visited many revival meetings in different places, obviously missed something and asks a very important question: Where is the fear of God? In all those Christian meetings he apparently couldn't find much of the fear of the Lord. How **timely** and **relevant** is the message that God gave us in His word for this time: "Fear God, and give glory to Him...worship Him that made heaven, and earth, and the sea, and the fountains of waters."

How appropriate for these days are the warnings of the second and the third angel! (Rev. 14:6–12) Let us proclaim this essential message of God, with great power, as a witness to all people!

To many there appears to be fear of the Lord and sincere worship of the Creator in the Alpha Course and in the Toronto movement, but in reality there are demonstrable occult bands and influences. *Bayith Ministries* in the UK published a book which reveals the different ties and influences from various occult, Jesuit, Freemason and New Age followers, with regard to the Alpha course and the Toronto blessing. *Bayith Ministries* has sent two open letters to Alpha to ask for an explanation. The first letter contains 16 documented questions. Three of the sixteen points are presented here:

> **7.** "Alpha teaches that the manifestations themselves don't matter, and that we should simply judge by the resulting fruit. Is this due to the absence of biblical support for these manifestations, and because of their amazing similarity to those things experienced in pagan religions such as the New Age movement?"
>
> **8.** "You cite John Wimber and his 1982 ministry team as be-

ing 'very significant' in your life. You quote Wimber regularly and glowingly, and you recommend his books. Do you not feel that such strong endorsement legitimizes the people whom he cited as being influential on him? These include: Morton Kelsey, Agnes Sanford, Kenneth Hagin, and John & Paula Sanford. Would you not agree that, in each case, their teachings are dangerous, and that they have admitted deriving aspects of their doctrine from New Agers? In view of verses like 1 Cor. 5:11 and Titus 3:10, are you not concerned about this, and about the fact that none of them have repented of their cooperation with such people?"

9. "Would you accept that Matthew 7:17–18 teaches us that the roots of a movement are very significant when determining if that movement is of God or not? Are you aware that Wimber largely attributed his 'anointing' to a man called Lonnie Frisbee who had been traveling with him for 18 months prior to Wimber's team ministering to you in 1982? Are you aware that Lonnie Frisbee worked with Bob Mumford and Kathryn Kuhlman during the 1970's? What do you think of them, given that they too derived much from New Agers?"

"Lonnie Frisbee, who was a practicing bisexual, died of AIDS in 1993, and is buried at Crystal Cathedral."

The letter with 16 questions challenging the integrity among the leaders of the revival movement was sent on April 4, 2003. Nicky Gumbel's secretary confirmed receiving it on April 9, but no attempt has been made to answer it or in any way to refute the things written. On November 12, 2003 a new letter was sent with 21 clearly presented questions, based on statements and quotations from the Alpha material requesting explanations concerning contradictions to the Bible. The following three points are a sample of the questions asked:

1. Hindered by prayer?

"You rightly say that 'The New Testament exhorts us to pray **'always'** (1 Thessalonians 5:17; Ephesians 6:18)', and, as you will be aware, other passages which teach us to pray without ceasing include Luke 18:1 and Luke 21:36. In light of these verses, can you explain why John Arnott—the head of the church that dispensed 'Toronto'—said the following words at HTB in 1995: 'Another thing that **hinders** [the Toronto Blessing] is, people **pray** all the time…Our experience is, that will hinder **substantially** your ability to receive…Pray **on the way out**; you can pray **later**'? Do we not distance God from the proceedings when we stop praying?"

16. Any precedent?

"HTB regularly cites Charles Finney and his ministry as a favourite precedent for Toronto-type experiences. Are you not aware that, towards the end of his life, Finney said of his followers, 'the great body of them are a **disgrace**'? Can you name any event in the Bible (or even any moment in the history of the true Church) which possessed the same attributes as the TE did? In other words, do you know of a single precedent for a genuine outpouring which: (a) was hindered by prayer, (b) was transferable, (c) increased when the teaching decreased, (d) produced manifestations which are all associated with hypnotism and apostasy, (e) was not a revival, (f) was Spirit-centred rather than Christ-centred, and (g) was rooted in doctrines and people who were plainly occultic? (We come from a Pentecostal background, yet we know of none.)"

21. Alpha related?

"If, as you imply, a 'milder' form of Toronto has been present at HTB since the eighties, would it not be fair to assume that the modern Alpha Course is at least partly a tool for bringing people into the TE? [Toronto Experience] Would you accept that numerous Alpha statements promote Toronto-type experiences and that many official testimonies reflect this? Can you tell us what the essential differences are between the manifestations on Alpha's 'Holy Spirit weekend' and those from 'Toronto'? Even if the 'more **intense**' experiences are not frequently seen on Alpha now, what fundamental difference does this represent? Is it not simply a return to the subtler version from HTB's past? Would you not agree that they have been shown to have identical roots? Are they not from the same spiritual source?"

A request for an answer to reasonable questions is normal. A short reply without any significant information in answer to the questions asked, came on December 1, 2003. The letter was called a "bizarre catalogue of suppositions and suggestions" and instead of providing some adequate answers they wrote:

All we can do in response is to encourage your readers to investigate the Alpha material for themselves...Our vision is simply to present the gospel of Jesus Christ to a needy world—and why there is cause to rejoice that more than six million people have now done an Alpha course and many have found faith in Jesus Christ for the first time. (Elizabeth McDonald & Dusty Peterson, *Bayith Ministries*, UK.)

This vision, in itself, sounds good, but we still have to test all things, according to the Bible. Although the Alpha publications give little information about the extreme Toronto manifestations that can occur during the course, there are well-known sources that do. We read for example that people "grunt like a pig and bark like a dog." (*The Times*, May 11, 1996.)

Even various staff members in Nicky Gumbel's HTB church have expressed their doubts whether God is really present in their services or that there might be other powers active.

"Some of the manifestations...may be of the devil." (Mark Elsdon-Dew, Ed., *The Collection,* HTB publ., 1996, p. 212.) The Toronto experience "could be a 'demonic counterfeit.'" (Wallace Boulton, Ed., *The Impact of Toronto,* Monarch, 1995, Appendix 4.)

Another permanent fellow-worker of Nicky Gumbel said:

> If these are meant to be times of refreshment, how come many of the leaders I have spoken to are already exhausted? Something **must** be **wrong**. (David Hilborn, *A Chronicle of the Toronto Blessing and Related Events*, as publ., by the Evangelical Alliance, UK, Part 2, PDF version, p. 54.)

Mike Fearon says about two important leaders of the Toronto phenomenon: "Kenyon and Hagin's work stems...nakedly from the occult" and "Their theology is basically deist...This is the very basis of **witchcraft.**" (Fearon, *A Breath of Fresh Air*, Eagle, 1994, p. 109.)

But Nicky Gumbel and Sandy Millar, the leaders of the HTB church, both say that the believers don't need to know anything about the men who brought the "Toronto Blessing" to the world. (Hillborn, *op. cit.,* p. 136. Boulton, *op. cit.*, p. 83.)

The Bible encourages us to test everything and God's children are being compared to an open letter: "known and read of all men." (2 Cor. 3:2) But if we are not allowed to know anything about those who inaugurate us into a special spiritual experience, then there probably is something seriously wrong, that cannot bear the light of investigation.

Chapter 11

Toronto—Alpha—Willow Creek—Saddleback

There is an obvious link between the Toronto blessing, the Alpha course, the Willow Creek community, and the Saddleback Church. They go hand in hand.

Bill Hybels is the leader of the Willow Creek community, which has a lot of support worldwide. Robert Schuller was Bill Hybels' mentor.

Schuller introduced a plan for church-growth in America and Hybels worked out the principles and practiced them. No wonder Schuller regards Hybels as his own son. He writes:

> I am so proud of him…I think of him as a son. I think of him as one of the greatest things to happen in Christianity in our time…Bill Hybels is doing the best job of anybody I know. (G. A. Pritchard, *Willow Creek Seeker Services, Evaluating a New Way of Doing Church*, Baker Books, 1996, p. 56.)

But who is Robert Schuller, from whom Bill Hybels took the principles for church-growth on which the Willow Creek community was founded? Schuller is the host of a huge and well known television show in America: "Hour of Power" and he uses the humanistic and antichristian "Victor Frankl Logotherapy". Schuller, in turn is a follower of Norman Vincent Peale, who plainly admitted that many of his principles came from two leading occultists: Ernest Holmes, founder of "Religious Science" and Charles Fillmore, co-founder of "Unity cult". (Dave Hunt, *Occult Invasion*, Eugene, Oregon, 1998, p. 460.)

Recently, it also became clear that the teachings of Norman Peale do have many remarkable resemblances with a third occult source: Florence Scovel Shinn, who drew her wisdom from mystic sources, that can be dated all the way back to the old Egyptian philosopher Hermes Trismegistus, and to the secrets of Freemasonry as they are described in the "Kybalion". (Ibid.)

The works of Shinn are republished with a foreword by Norman Peale, and are available at New Age bookstores. Vincent Norman Peale and Robert Schuller are, after all, both 33rd degree Freemasons. It is therefore not surprising that many serious Christians experience great difficulty with the present church-growth movement that seems to conquer the world. (Ibid. p. 461.)

Bill Hybels, Rick Warren, Nicky Gumbel, and almost all church-growth and revival leaders have in mind the merging of all churches, spiritual and religious groups, and movements. From this point of view Bill Hybels invited a Muslim leader, Fred Hammouda, to speak to Willow Creek's community about Islam.

> Hammouda was provided with this huge forum to spread lies about his false and dangerous religion. He blamed the U.S. for recent terrorism and professed hate for the U.S. and Israel. (*Bill Hybels, General Teachings/Activities, Biblical Discernment Ministries,* 2/2004, p. 14.)

F. M. Laz, a Roman Catholic priest of the "Holy Family Church", was also invited by Hybels to make clear in the Willow Creek Church the things that Protestants can learn from Catholics. As he introduced Laz, Bill Hybels told that he was invited at a conference to speak in the Holy Family Church for a group of Catholic leaders, and that he had gained much admiration and respect for Laz as a brother in Christ. (Audiotape M9010 *WC Seeds Tape Ministry.*)

Bill Hybels admitted that he couldn't agree on every point of the Catholic faith, but the differences were too small to name; and he told the listeners that they could learn from the Catholic Church—and he seemed to have nothing but praise.

We read:

> ...the opinion is gaining ground that, after all, we do not differ so widely upon vital points as has been supposed, and that a little concession on our part will bring us into a better understanding with

Rome...The people need to be aroused to resist the advances of this most dangerous foe to civil and religious liberty. (E. G. White, *The Great Controversy*, pp. 563, 566.)

Dave Hunt writes:

God said, 'My people are destroyed for lack of knowledge' (Hosea 4:6). Tragically, Christian leaders who ought to be providing, along with the truth of God's Word, the factual knowledge that would help to keep evangelicals from today's ecumenical delusion are withholding it. (*Occult Invasion*, Harvest House Publ., Eugene, Oregon, 1998, p. 586.)

Today, the public statements of the Vatican are making it clear that unity is being sought on Rome's own terms. Rome is using the Evangelical Movement as a ploy both to entice professed Protestants and to weaken their churches. Then full blown Romanism is demanded, with just a few superficial concessions, as the terms of union... where Rome is in control and democracy is weak or nonexistent, a policy of persecution is followed...despite all the Ecumenical statements made to the wider world by the Vatican. (I. A. Sadler, *Mystery, Babylon the Great*, Cromwell Press, UK, 2003, pp. 242, 243.)

He who thinks that Rome, during the last decades, has become more gentle and guarantees now freedom of religion, should read Alan Campbell's recent booklet: *Blood Behind The Purple Curtain, Horrific Evidence That Rome Still Persecutes Today.* The facts of 28 cases of terror are presented.

...the Roman Hierarchy is demanding new harsh legislation against the Evangelicals. Yet here in Britain, they speak of unity, love and reconciliation...the fact is that where Rome has power, she still persecutes today. (*Open-Bible Ministries,* P.O. Box 92, Belfast.)

Says Ellen White: "The pacific tone of Rome...does not imply a change of heart. She is tolerant where she is helpless." (*The Great Controversy*, p. 565.)

In an apostolic letter: *Ad Tuendam Fidem,* May 18, 1998, the pope made an appeal to protect the Catholic faith. And canon 1436.1, proclaims: "One who denies a truth which must be believed with divine and Catholic faith, or who calls it into doubt...**is to be punished as a heretic or an apostate** with major excommunication..." (Emphasis added.)

Roman Catholic doctrine is unalterable.

The Catholic Church did not change any of its doctrines at Trent and it did not change any at Vatican II. (Karl Keating, *Catholicism and Fundamentalism*, Ignatius Press, San Francisco, 1988, p. 103.)

...there are many indications that Rome is fundamentally the same as it has always been." (Schrotenboer, ed. *Roman Catholicism: A Contemporary Evangelical Perspective*, p. 7.) "Roman Catholicism does not change. At heart, it is the same as it ever was. (John Philipps, *Can a Christian remain a Roman Catholic?* p. 31.)

Let none deceive themselves. The papacy that Protestants are now so ready to honor is the same that ruled the world in the days of the Reformation... (*The Great Controversy*, p. 571.)

It is, however, even more tragic when Christian leaders betray the gospel, while they pretend to believe it. During the "Phil Donahue" campaign, back in 1984, Norman Vincent Peale, for example, said: "It's not necessary to be born again. You have your way to God; I have mine. I found eternal peace in a Shinto shrine...I've been to Shinto shrines, and God is everywhere."

Shocked by this, Phil Donahue responded, "But you're a Christian minister; you're supposed to tell me that Christ is the way and the truth and the life, aren't you?" Peale replied, "Christ is one of the ways. God is everywhere." (*Christian News*, May 12, 1997, p. 11.)

Such are the devices of the modern church-growth and revival movement, whereby every kind of religion and spirituality should feel at home, and on which they should unite.

Chapter 12

Alpha Conference

At the Anglican St. Matthew's Church, Sherwood, Brisbane, Australia, an Alpha Conference was held in June 1998. The editor of *Despatch* magazine was there during the entire conference and made a report.

Although the atmosphere was kind and pleasant, this editor feels it would be unthinkable and loveless not to warn. Could Alpha be a tool of the enemy? We read: "Yet that is what it is! A very deceptive, attractive delusion yes, but a trap perpetrated by the enemy of the Cross!" (Wendy B. Howard, *The Alpha Course—Friend or Foe? Information gathered from "The Alpha Conference"* 1998, p. 4.)

The beginning is quite good, but as the course progresses, the experiences of the HTB (mother church of the Alpha course) concerning the Toronto blessing are brought up more and more. Incorrect explanations are given of different Bible passages and appeals are made for unity in an atmosphere of over emphasis on the Holy Spirit. This is all so typical of Toronto followers. The whole idea is apparently to gather in unity as many people and religions together as possible. The Toronto phenomenon is the binding factor to make sure that the whole group will be led by one spirit.

What is the real main aim of Alpha? Is it the pure proclamation of the gospel of Jesus Christ or is the gospel repeatedly referred to only to hide its real agenda and calm the doubts of those who are suspicious it is not what it pretends to be? Although it professes to be primarily about the preaching of the gospel, it is evident that achieving the unity of all churches by the ecumenical movement is the great objective of Alpha international.

> ...the overall impression coming from Alpha internationally is that UNITY through the ecumenical movement is the purpose of Alpha. UNITY, with the Vatican in control is the ultimate purpose of Alpha. (Ibid., p. 5.)

Mona Carter, the Australian Alpha leader, spoke about a "vision" she had received in which Jesus stood in the middle of a "burning fire" which rushed across the country into every church and fellowship. Alpha across the world. Alpha across the whole of Australia...

> The false 'revival fire' of the Toronto curse was very present at the quiet, dignified conference. Toronto revival and extreme experiences were lauded by both speakers, Bruce Sligo and Mona Carter. Bruce Sligo talked of the experience he had had of an electric shock-like jolt laid on by hands at the Brompton home of Alpha in the UK. Both speakers had gone at various times to the UK to catch the Alpha bug. This is a huge international movement, frighteningly deceptive, which is breaking down barriers across the globe. Sligo spoke of the changes going on in the world, of the need to move into the PARADIGM SHIFT of a global experience-seeking world, out of the 'enlightenment' mentality of stressing cognitive, doctrinal understanding. All this is NEW AGE oriented! Alpha is a movement of the New Age spirit of our times into the UNITY of all religions in a One World Church. (Ibid., p. 5.)

If you have doubts, then just read the messages about the many Alpha activities that are taking place around the world in so many different religions.

Here's just one testimony:

> "I've made friends on Alpha with Catholics and Protestants—there's a bond nothing can break." "Alpha was 'like the sun coming out on an otherwise dull day'—it breathed new life." "Alpha...is being seen as a means of drawing together both Protestants and Catholics..." "Alpha bids to focus on common ground." (*Alpha News* March–July, 1998, p. 10, 11.)

No one needs to question Alpha's objective. Differences do not count. On the principle of common ground Protestants and Catholics should unite.

Alpha refers to the Roman Catholic Church more frequently—

and more positively—than to any other religious body. This must surely influence Course participants when they come to choose a church. Despite the dangers of Rome's interfaith stance, Alpha invariably speaks *very* highly of her... There are many glowing references to Rome—plus numerous quotes from prominent Catholics—throughout the Alpha talks and in related publications. For example, one issue of *Alpha News* [Mar–Jun 2000] devoted its largest article to the subject of Catholic-run Alpha Courses and, in the same issue, another page was given over to the view of two Catholic bishops. (Elizabeth McDonald and Dusty Peterson, *Alpha the unofficial guide,* St. Matthew Publ., Cambridge, UK, 2004, p. 23.)

Note how Nicky Gumbel supports Catholic doctrine:

> Peter of course was...the one of whom Jesus said, "On this rock I will build my Church." So Peter became this great figure in the Christian Church. (*Talk 12, Why and How Should We Tell Others?* Video set.)

Alpha News even carried an advert, entitled "Catholic Follow-Up to Alpha" for fifteen supplementary videos. (March–July, 2000, p. 17. Cf., *Alpha the unofficial guide, p. 40.*)   Nicky Gumbel not only fails to warn against the specific unbiblical catholic teachings contained in these follow-up talks (such as "Why should I go to Mass?"), he even advertises them, thus lending official approval to these videos. This appears to be a more serious matter in the light of the following Catholic claims:

Although Rome refers to Protestants as "separated brethren" she claims to be "**the single** Church of Christ... governed by the **Successor of Peter**." (Cardinal Ratzinger [now being pope], *Dominus Iesus. On the Unicity and Salvific Universality of Jesus Christ and the Church.* Sept. 5, 2000. Emphasis added.) Note how the Protestant churches, in fact, are more or less eclipsed by the following claims:

> The Catholic Church possesses the **whole** of the wealth of God's revealed truth and **all** the means of grace. It is **unable** to concede **similar** status to others. (Cardinal Hume, *Towards a Civilisation of Love.* 1988. Emphasis added.)

Whosoever, therefore, knowing that the Catholic Church is

made necessary by God through Jesus Christ, would refuse to **enter her** or to **remain** in her **could not be saved**. (Vatican II, *Dogmatic Constitution on Divine Revelation,* 18 Nov., 1965, par. 14. Emphasis added.)

It is sad to notice that Nicky Gumbel and the Alpha Course neglect and undermine the mighty work of the divinely inspired revival of the Reformation. "…the Alpha Course is proving to be a most profitable vehicle for Rome's ecumenical goals." (E. McDonald & D. Peterson, *Alpha, the unofficial guide,* Cambridge, 2004, p. 55.)

But besides the offensive Catholic leanings there are other serious problems for sincere Christians with the Alpha Course.

The editor of *Despatch* magazine writes that there is often ambiguity. That which is clearly said doesn't always correspond with reality. Alpha doesn't bring a sound Biblical message although many who attended the conference will protect Alpha and say that a true and clear message is preached. On the contrary, Alpha strongly emphasizes experience, feeling, emotion, fun, visions, slaying in the spirit, the "fire" of revival, and such things. Meanwhile, there is apostasy of genuine truth and of Biblical doctrine.

We read:

> Without doubt the saddest result of the great 'falling away' of this present period of Church history is that the denominations have left many members with little, or no discernment about error, nor can they adequately evaluate the false teachings which are at flood level all through the churches! Alpha is a very clever counterfeit, which could well be one of the main tools which will be used to fit Pentecostals and evangelicals into the One World Church of the New World Order. (Howard, *The Alpha Course—Friend or Foe,* p. 6.)

Although the Alpha leaders stressed obedience and a relation with God, it was striking that solidarity with Alpha was emphasized more: "The commitment was to ALPHA, because we were told, ALPHA is the answer for the world, ALPHA is the tool in God's hands." (Ibid., p. 7.) This was argued with strong conviction.

But isn't Christ the only answer for this world? Isn't only He the Way, the Truth and the Life for all mankind? Wouldn't it be better to line up with God and trust ourselves with more dedication to Him? And wouldn't it be better if we didn't listen to Alpha, but to the will of God and make known the name of Jesus in the whole world? After all, the apostle Paul says: "For I am determined not to know anything among you, save Jesus Christ, and Him crucified." (1 Cor. 2:2) Jesus Christ – and not Alpha – is the central theme and the only answer for this wicked world "for there is none other name under heaven given among men, whereby we must be saved... Jesus Christ, who gave himself for our sins, that he might deliver us from this present evil world, according to the will of God and our Father, to whom be glory for ever and ever." (Acts 4:12; Gal. 1:3–5) Not Alpha, but Christ is the instrument in God's hand for true church-growth, since to Him is given "according to the will of God" to "deliver us from this present evil world." Christ and Christ alone, in harmony with Scripture, has to be our focus in church-growth activities.

Alpha deviates from God's Word. Alpha is a tool in the hand of the ecumenical movement. Alpha works together with everybody who calls himself religious, irrespective of God's advice not to form a co-operating alliance with those that support wrong doctrines. Everyone is encouraged to unite in brotherhood and not to care about the differences of doctrine, but to pay attention to the things that unite.

Alpha doesn't preach God's End time message and neither does it proclaim a necessary warning against the existing dangers of the last days in which we now live. Alpha just speaks about unity, revival, and church-growth and not about the apostasy which the Bible mentions. Alpha proclaims that the teachings are subordinate and that the doctrines are less important, while the Bible clearly states that soundness of doctrine is necessary and deserves all attention. The proclamation of unadulterated doctrines is a characteristic of God's true church, for only by the truth is man sanctified and truly set free.

Alpha assumes that the manifesting power of the Spirit will take control of sinners who are not born again, although the Bible makes clear that the power of the Spirit will be manifested in sincere believers with a newborn and dedicated heart. Alpha teaches that the spiritual birth is a process that takes a whole lifetime to make it as complete as can be. But that is in harmony with Catholic opinion and not in line with what the Bible teaches.

The spiritual birth takes place when penitent sinners willingly and obediently accept Jesus Christ with sincere faith. The moment of rebirth into a new spiritual life is the moment when the sinner is justified by faith through Jesus Christ and through Him has become a child of God, called to a new life of sanctification, and **that** is the process of a lifetime. Alpha and the Catholic Church don't present a clear biblical picture since not the rebirth but sanctification is the process of a lifetime.

Chapter 13

Seeker Friendly

The practice of Alpha is that all glory is given to unbelieving sinners who aren't redeemed. They need to be approached in an affirmative and respectful manner and be in no way confronted. They need to be listened to and everything that can be disturbing or hurting to them by word or act must be avoided because the first requirement is that they should feel perfectly comfortable. The program or service must—without question—be pleasant, interesting, and agreeable, and everything possible has to be done to make everybody feel happy. Tasteful meals are served and a nice atmosphere of being together is created.

While it is true that we must be courteous and thoughtful to all, showing an interest in each, we must avoid flattery and/or anything that would hinder the work of the Spirit, Whose first work is to convict of sin: "When the Spirit of truth" is come, He will reprove the world of sin, and of [Christ's] righteousness, and of Judgment to come." (John 16:8.)

Instead of flattery, God's plan is that we focus upon His love for each and His longing to accept all who come to Christ as the Great High Priest.

This divine objective is strongly objected to in the Alpha program to which the Spirit's three fold mission is not acceptable. Not one of these would be accepted in the Alpha program. Reproof for sin directly violates its rules. Moreover focusing upon Christ's righteousness is the most effective way of arousing a sense of guilt and desire to repent. And of course, consciousness of a "judgment to come " only raises the intensity of concern that calls for repentance. Thus, instead of the progressive truth of which the Spirit seeks to convict, contemporary, popular music is played. Nor does it matter whether it is beat, jazz, or rock. No, the purpose is to please and satisfy the visitors, and this is done by giving them what they want and are used to hearing. **A brief, relevant message is to be preached, with which everyone can easily agree, while preaching on dogmatic issues and doctrines is not allowed and regarded as boring. Modern marketing principles are recommended and the unbelieving sinner has to be regarded as a customer and be treated as a king. He has to be drawn in a pleasant manner, gripped, and held fast by all sorts of modern and lively presentations, making use of professional technical means.**

But, however pleasant and seemingly useful, should we respect those charming appearances as is expected?

> The religion of Christ needs not such attractions to recommend it. In the light shining from the cross, true Christianity appears so pure and lovely that no external decorations can enhance its true worth. It is the beauty of holiness, a meek and quiet spirit, which is of value with God…A religion of externals is attractive to the unrenewed heart. (*The Great Controversy,* pp. 566, 567.)

Instructions are given by Alpha, how to deal with unchurched people:

> One of the standard rules for small group dialogue tells members to respect every diverse position or point of view. Don't violate someone's comfort zone by implying that an unbiblical behavior or lifestyle constitutes sin. (Berit Kjos, April 9, 2004, Part 9, *Dealing with Resisters*, p. 53.)

This modern approach must not be confused with common courtesy and thoughtfulness which should characterize relations to all people. But Alpha's aim, rather, is to avoid issues of truth so as to bring about a satisfied feeling within people. Is this God's way to lead lost sinners to humbly and penitently come to Christ? Would this not, rather stimulate a deceptive feeling of self-righteousness and self-esteem without a clear perception of the necessity to lead a newborn life in Christ like the Bible tells us?

Aren't lost sinners rather soothed and kept busy in an agreeable way by this honorable, elegant and royal approach of Alpha, giving a feeling that there isn't much wrong with them? Would they not then rather lead a superficial Christian life instead of experiencing sincere repentance? No responsible leader in God's service, who has His Word as his standard, could ever with impunity neglect to present a sound picture of sin, repentance, conversion, rebirth, and true redemption in Christ Jesus by living a pure and holy life in obedience to God's law.

Is it ever a faithful proclamation of the Biblical doctrines to make the natural man feel better without repentance and surrender so as to live a camouflaged, outward Christian life? Is it ever safe to leave sinners without a right Biblical conception and solution of his depraved sinful nature? Is it loving to leave one in ignorance concerning his pitiful situation and not to call him to unconditional and total surrender? Is it strange then, that Charles Finney, who is set as an example by Alpha, had to admit about his followers that most of them were a stain?

Finney, who indeed had many good things, considered a pleasant and happy feeling as the main aim and he regarded the rebirth not as an action of the Spirit, but of the human will. (*The New Schaff-Herzorg Encycl.* vol. VI, p. 317.) This is obviously a tangent, for Alpha also stresses the human possibilities and will.

Is it possible for the natural man to reveal the power of redemption and change of his sinful nature? If lost sinners are led to trust in themselves for their salvation and spiritual life and cherish feelings of self-esteem, can we then expect them to be sincerely converted souls, who faithfully reveal the fruit of the Spirit in their lives?

The apostle Paul clearly writes: "Not that we are sufficient of ourselves to think any thing as of ourselves; but our sufficiency is of God." (2 Cor. 3:5)

But the church-growth movement presents an attractive gospel that caters to carnal desires. The Bible should be presented in a friendly manner, but though its principles are sometimes reflected, often a picture is outlined contrary to what the Bible says, but which is more appealing to modern man. The primary purpose is to make everybody feel comfortable. But Paul writes plainly: "for if I yet pleased men, I should not be the servant of Christ." (Gal. 1:10. Cf., 1 Thess. 2:4)

Ignoring this principle, church-growth leaders do everything possible to please men. Indeed, a clear, "thus saith the Lord" is ruled out by the mandate that everybody must feel comfortable with everything that is said!

Howard speaks about ambiguity and Busenitz makes clear that though Hybels and Warren have written a rather good message, "in practice, they de-emphasize certain parts of orthodox theology." Kimon Howland states: "seeker church pastors make orthodox theology less offensive and more civil for a pluralistic society." The gospel isn't put aside but repacked "in a kinder, gentler format." (Nathan Busenitz, *The Gospel According to Hybels & Warren*, Pulpit-Shepherds' Fellowship, 2003, p. 3, 4.)

Os Guinness declares:

> When megachurch pastors seek to mold a message to their 'market' of constituent needs their preaching omits key components. Gone are the hard sayings of Jesus. Gone is the teaching on sin, self-denial, sacrifice, suffering, judgment, hell. With all its need-meeting emphases, there is little in the church-growth movement that stands crosswise to the world. (Os Guinness, *Dining with the Devil*, Baker Book, 1993, p. 78.)

Busenitz concludes:

> Sadly, by watering-down the message and using unbiblical methods, CGM [church-growth movement] and its seeker sensitive counterparts may be doing more harm than good—filling their auditoriums with vast crowds of lost people who think they're spiritually okay…Having investigated both its evangelistic message and its evangelistic model, the sad conclusion is that the gospel according to Hybels and Warren falls far short of the biblical paradigm. (Busenitz, op. cit., p. 16.)

Dave who studied with his church Rick Warren's book: *The Purpose Driven Life*, writes:

> There are some really good things and points that Rick Warren brings out. But they always seem to be mixed with so many confusing and theologically weak points that you go crazy trying to keep it all straight…Dave speaks for a multitude of troubled people. While Pastor Warren's manual on Christian living has captivated churches

around the world, a rising number of discerning readers question its subtle distortions, its half-truths, its conflicting messages and its pragmatic permissiveness: if it works (i.e. brings people into the church), it's okay! "God loves variety!" (Berit Kjos, *Spirit-led or Purpose driven?* Part 1, October 9, 2003, NewsWithViews.com p. 1.)

In a Baptist newsletter we read about Willow Creek:

Bill Hybels is one of the most dangerous religious leaders in America. Through his ministry at Willow Creek Community Church, South Barrington, Illinois, and the Willow Creek Association, **he is leading many Baptists** into the web of compromise. **Churches are being destroyed**, while at the same time they are growing in membership. If this seems to be a contradiction, just remember that when a church departs from the faith it is destroyed, no matter how many members they may continue to have. Every Sunday morning about 15,000 people gather in the Willow Creek Community Church (WCCC). This is not your regular church service. There is no organ, piano, hymnbooks. They do not join in singing the grand old hymns of the Christian faith. Neither is there a biblical sermon preached. This is their so-called **Seeker Service**, which is produced in order **to get lost people to enjoy church without guilt or shame**. There are **no sermons against sin, nor** is there a call for **repentance**. Instead of this, there is plenty of rock music from a rock band. Instead of a biblical sermon **they feature dramas and multi-media**. Of course, the lost man likes to be entertained, and he gets plenty of that at WCCC. (*International Social Pulse Newsletter*, Nov. 2003, *Bapt. Churches caught in Willow Creek Web.* Emphasis in original.)

Chapter 14

Another Gospel

One of the remarkable things is that Rick Warren makes much use of a modern Bible, with its paraphrased meaning.

> It's not surprising that Pastor Warren quotes passages from *The Message* (a paraphrased "version" of the Bible by Eugene Peterson) over ninety times. Many of those simplified passages alter both the words and the meaning of the Scriptures. But they fit the points Pastor Warren is trying to make. (Berit Kjos, Part 3, *Softening God's Word*, 2003, p. 10.)

Warren however says that we often miss the full meaning of the known verses. "Therefore I have deliberately used paraphrases in order to help you see God's truth in new, fresh ways." (*The Purpose Driven Life*, p. 325.)

This sounds good, but this also makes it possible to adapt the Bible to one's opinion. We read for instance: "But the hour cometh, and now is, when the true worshippers shall worship the Father in spirit and in truth: for the Father seeketh such to worship Him." (John 4:23)

Consider *The Message* version: "That's the kind of people the Father is out looking for: those who are simply and honestly themselves before him in worship."

This version suits Warren well for his church-growth program that doesn't emphasize worshipping in truth. No, everybody needs to feel at ease, whatever his opinion or way of thinking; and no one is allowed to address issues of true or false doctrine. Thus Warren deliberately avoids the clear call for true worshippers to confess the truth in their worship by this very different, adapted version that, instead of "worship in spirit and in truth" speaks of being "simply and honestly themselves" in worship. This is but one of many places where Warren's books dishonour the Bible.

Fundamental, Biblical concepts are formulated and Bible passages explained in a way that suits the modern man, and makes it easier to accept. For example, Robert Schuller, the instructor of Bill Hybels of Willow Creek, writes: "Sin is any act or thought that robs myself or another human being of his or her self-esteem." (Schuller, *Self Esteem, The New Reformation*, Word Books, Waco, Texas, 1982, p. 14.)

Scripture, however, doesn't speak in terms of self-esteem but simply tells us that sin is disobedience and violation of God's law.

The Bible teaches that we should not cherish our own ego—we should crucify our own self. But Schuller assures: "The Cross sanctifies the ego trip." (Ibid., p. 75.)

He even writes:

> I don't think anything has been done in the name of Christ and under the banner of Christianity that has proven more destructive to human personality and, hence, counterproductive to the evangelism enterprise than the often crude, uncouth, and unchristian strategy of attempting to make people aware of their lost and sinful condition. (*Christianity Today*, Oct. 5, 1984.)

In another place Schuller declares:

> The most serious sin is the one that causes me to say, "I am unworthy"…The fact is, the church will never succeed until it satisfies the human being's hunger for self-value. (Dr. Cathy Burns, *Billy Graham and his Friends*, p. 114.)

And as for the prayer Jesus taught us to pray, Schuller blasphemously declares: "And we can pray, 'Our Father in heaven, honorable is **our** name." He then adds: "So the foundation is laid for us to feel good about ourselves!" (Schuller, *Self Esteem, The New Reformation*, Word Books, Waco, Texas, 1982, p. 69.)

Schuller feels at home with every religion. When in 1987 the pope visited Los Angeles, Schuller said: "It's time for Protestants to go to the shepherd (or the Pope) and say, 'What do we have to do to come home?'" (*Omega-Letter*, March 1998, vol. 3, no. 3, p. 15.)

Schuller invites many persons of different religious background to appear in his shows. These include Muslims, Catholics, Mormons, New Agers, Freemasons, and Satanists! "Schuller teaches there is no need for one to recognize his own personal sin, no need for repentance, and no need for the crucifixion of self." Everybody is good! (Burns, *Billy Graham and his Friends*, pp. 113–120. Underlining in original.) Schuller's influence is noticeable in the church-growth movement. Sinful human beings need to be carried along and everybody has to be very careful in dealing with those persons not to hurt their feelings by confronting them with their own lost, sinful condition. Schuller clearly emphasizes human self-esteem, dignity, and abilities and he wants to convince everybody:

> …that you can if you think you can…by realizing the amazing possibilities inherent in the mind. (David L. Smith, *A Handbook of Contemporary Theology,* 1992, p. 189.)

This whole idea has more in common with the New Age movement than with the Bible. The occult cosmic Christ who will come and rule the world calls everyone to put to use the creative powers and possibilities hidden in every person. New Ager, Matthew Fox urges:

> Find the creative person, the "I am," the divine child at play and a generativity in your self. Give birth to yourself—your lifestyles, your relationships, your learning, your sexuality, your joys, your healing, your work—and build up in one another this same courage to create…Do not bore me by refusing. Do not scandalize me by saying "I can't." (*The Coming of the Cosmic Christ,* Harper & Row, San Francisco, 1988, p. 211.)

This unbiblical approach of personal abilities and self-esteem encourages sinful humans to trust in themselves and feel capable of their own redemption. And this precludes the possibility of experiencing a genuine spiritual rebirth; for how can we meet together and worship God with such a feeling of self-esteem?

It is idolatrous to worship with a feeling of self-esteem, selfishness, and covetousness. Our need is to learn Christ's humility and meekness, as He has taught us we should. (Matt. 11:29)

> There should be a solemn awe upon the worshipers…for it is the place where God reveals His presence…therefore pride and

passion, dissension and self-esteem, selfishness, and covetousness, which God pronounces idolatry, are inappropiate for such a place. (E. G. White, *Child Guidance*, p. 543.)

Gumbel, Warren, and Hybels are following the path of Schuller's man-centered and man-directed New Age gospel. Of this psychological approach of Willow Creek G. A. Pritchard states:

…instead of encouraging Creekers to know and love God, [it] encourages them to know and accept themselves and develop a strong self-esteem. The goals and means of one's ethics change from a God-centered to a human-centered orientation. (G. A. Pritchard, *Willow Creek Seeker Services,* Baker Books, 1996, p. 234.)

Gumbel writes:

The good news is that with the help of the Spirit we can change. The Holy Spirit gives us freedom to live the sort of lives that deep down, we have always wanted to live... (*Why Jesus?* p. 13.)

Yes, indeed, the Spirit does give us freedom to live the sort of lives which He inspires, 'deep down.' But the Spirit does not give us the freedom to live according to the carnal desires of our own heart, as we always wanted to. No, He wants to **recreate** us with a completely **new** heart. In ourselves we are sinful and stand at enmity against righteousness and a sanctified life. In order to be saved we need to be born again and receive a completely new life-principle through the washing of regeneration, and renewal of the Holy Spirit. (Cf. Titus 3:5)

According to Warren, everybody can be quite easily won for Christ.

Warren says, "…anybody can be won to Christ if you discover the felt needs to his or her heart." Warren says that all people need to do is whisper a sweet prayer to Jesus and they "will" be saved, 'quietly whisper the prayer that will change your eternity: "Jesus, I believe in you and I receive you."' (C. Matthew McMahon, *Pelagian Captivity,* p. 19. Cf., *The Purpose Driven Church.* p. 219; *The Purpose Driven Life,* p. 58.)

According to the Bible, we are not saved by the human will or our own abilities or anything we must discover by or within ourselves

(Rom. 9:16). No, Jesus clearly declares: "No man can come to me, except the Father which hath sent me draw him" (John 6:44).

Our eternity will only change when we are born "not of blood, nor of the will of the flesh, nor of the will of man, but of God." (John 1:13)

Hybels explains:

> We are a love starved people, with broken parts that need the kind of repair that only he can give long-term. We need to bring our brokenness out into the light of his grace and truth. (C. Matthew McMahon, *Pelagian Captivity*, pp. 19, 20.)

The unbeliever is by his own nature not merely broken. No, he is **dead** in trespasses and sins. Thus healing is not sufficient; he must be raised from death unto a **newborn life**. This is what the Bible says. We read:

> You... who were dead in trespasses and sins... were by nature... children of wrath... But God, who is rich in mercy, for his great love wherewith he loved us, even when we were dead in sins hath quickened us together... in Christ Jesus... For by grace are ye saved through faith; and that not of yourselves: it is the gift of God: not of works, lest any man should boast. For we are his workmanship, created in Christ Jesus unto good works. (Eph. 2:1–10)

Those who are dead cannot accomplish anything; they possess no spiritual capacity. They need resurrection life. They are called to life in and with Christ, for He alone has conquered death. Salvation is in no way of ourselves. Only as new creatures, created in Christ Jesus, can we be saved and do good. That is the pure and sane Biblical message! We must not let anybody put us on a wrong track by cherishing feelings of self-esteem, believing there are unknown possibilities and divine powers in our selves that could accomplish our salvation and give us the ability to live a good and obedient life. For this just leads to a great disappointment, of which the apostle Paul testifies: Now if I do that I would not, it is no more I that do it, but sin that dwelleth in me." Then he says in despair: "O wretched man that I am! Who shall deliver me from the body of this death?" (Rom. 7:20, 24)

Alpha actually hinders sinners from experiencing the power of the gospel by encouraging them to believe they are Christians, while they haven't given themselves fully to God. Alpha's attempts to truly bring people to Christ as their Redeemer, are thus contrary to the light of the gospel. Concerning this W. B. Howard says: "all effort will be given to the Alpha trip!" (*The Alpha Course, Friend or Foe?* p. 11.)

Chapter 15

Inaccuracies

Although the Alpha Course and Warren's books contain good things, there are also a lot of alarming passages with incorrect, unbiblical, or doubtful information, usually cleverly and inconspicuously presented. However, careful study will surely reveal to the attentive and knowledgeable reader the misleading dangers.

Gary E. Gilley, Pastor-teacher, Southern View Chapel, Springfield IL, writes in his review of Warren's book *The Purpose Driven Life*, that has become a much favoured study object in many churches, worldwide:

> As I began reading this book, the problems were so numerous and obvious that I backed up and began marking these errors. I found 42 such biblical inaccuracies, plus 18 out-of-context passages of Scripture, supposedly used to prove his point, and another 9 distorted translations…In general, there is much that is disturbing within the pages of '*The Purpose-Driven Life.*' Even though he denies it, Warren is obviously a disciple of pop-psychology, which is littered throughout…
>
> Our concern here is focused on his blatant twisting of the biblical text to suit his purposes. This is a dangerous trend that will lead to nothing good if not recognized, challenged, and rejected by the Christian community…
>
> So, what difference does it make? What if Warren is misrepresenting Scripture over 40 times as well as peppering his book with extra-biblical psychological theories and other earthly pieces of wisdom, disguised as biblical principles?…

But of a more serious nature is this careless and wanton mishandling of Scripture...To purposely ignore the proper translation of a passage and insert one that has no basis in the original languages in order to under gird a particular point of view is about the most dangerous thing that I can imagine. The only thing more concerning would be to discover large segments of the evangelical community being incapable of discerning this kind of problem—and / or not caring...

Warren, however, is not totally off base...Nevertheless, when every third page (on average) of a book presents either an unbiblical, or at least a biblically unsupported idea, there is not much sense bothering to read it. And that would be my suggestion—don't bother. (*The Church Growth Movement*...Compiled by Japie Grobler, pp. 16, 22. Kies Ciec, P.O. Box 8009, Edleen 1625, Africa.)

It is remarkable that besides mis-presenting Scriptural information, Warren also freely quotes people with occultic and New Age backgrounds. On page 30 of *The Purpose Driven Life*, for instance, Warren writes about the benefits of purpose-driven living and quotes Isaiah and Job as if they had no purpose in their lives, while on the next page he quotes Dr. Bernie Siegel.

Without God, life has no purpose, and without purpose, life has no meaning. Without meaning, life has no significance or hope. In the Bible, many different people expressed this hopelessness. Isaiah complained, "I have labored to no purpose; I have spent my strength in vain and for nothing." Job said, "My life drags by—day after hopeless day" and "I give up; I am tired of living. Leave me alone. My life makes no sense." The greatest tragedy is not death, but life without purpose.

Was Isaiah's **life** without purpose, as Warren seems to suggest? If we read the quoted passage in its context, we realize that it is not about Isaiah's life as such, but about his God given task "to bring Jacob again to him." (Isaiah 49:5). In **that** context of being God's servant, while recognizing "my work (is) with my God," Isaiah says, "I have laboured in vain, I have spent my strength for nought, and in vain." Isaiah said so, not because he had no purpose in his personal life, but because his **message** remained without effect, as the people did not listen.

> He well knew that he would encounter obstinate resistance. As he…thought of the stubbornness and unbelief of the people for whom he was to labour, his task seemed hopeless. (E. G. White, *Prophets and Kings*, p. 307.)

Although his task seemed hopeless, Isaiah was not without hope and purpose in his life, nor even as to his task, for, despite the unwillingness of the people in his days, the prophet knew that at last, in after years, his message would bear fruit. And so Isaiah could with a "purpose driven life" and with a "purpose driven" task, hopefully and courageously perform his mission, as a called servant of God.

> This assurance of the final fulfillment of God's purpose brought courage to the heart of Isaiah…For sixty years or more he stood before the children of Judah as a prophet of hope, waxing bolder and still bolder in his predictions of the future triumph of the church. (Ibid., p. 310.)

Although "error and superstition flourished…when he was called to the prophetic mission; yet he was not discouraged, for ringing in his ears was the triumphal chorus of the angels surrounding the throne of God, 'The whole earth is full of His glory.' Isaiah 6:3. And his faith was strengthened by visions of glorious conquests by the church of God." (Ibid., p. 371.)

The prophet Isaiah, in the midst of the ruling darkness, seeing no positive result of his mission in his days, is a unique example of unusual hope and courage and unflinching singleness of purpose.

But Rick Warren not only ignores this, but even suggests the opposite. Moreover he quotes Job with the same intention. Can we agree that Job didn't have any purpose in his life? Unfortunately, Warren does not make a difference between Job's physical life and his spiritual life. Because of the great agony of physical suffering he had to endure, it is perfectly understandable that he had, this way, a problem with his life and says: "I loathe it; I would not live alway: let me alone; for my days are vanity." (Job. 7:16.)

While his prospect of recovery was veiled, Job didn't understand why he had to suffer so much. But does this also mean that Job, spiritually, was without hope and purpose?

From the depths of discouragement and despondency Job rose to the heights of implicit trust in the mercy and the saving power of God. Triumphantly he declared: 'Though He slay me, yet will I trust in Him:...He also shall be my salvation.' 'I know that my Redeemer liveth, And that He shall stand at the latter day upon the earth: And though after my skin worms destroy this body, Yet in my flesh shall I see God: Whom I shall see for myself, And mine eyes shall behold, and not another.' Job 13:15, 16; 19:25-27. (E. G. White, *Prophets and Kings,* pp. 163, 164.)

Here now, we have Job's unwavering hope, implicit faith and firm trust in God. Was Job without purpose in his lamentable suffering? Surely not! He kept his eye fixed on a righteous reward. He was convinced of coming salvation. He knew that he would, at the latter day, see his Redeemer with his own eyes. That was his firm purpose that nobody could take away from him.

Job's "purpose-driven" perseverance in his much afflicted life is just a very unique and powerful witness for all who meet with suffering, despondency and misfortune.

No wonder the Bible reminds us of Job's patience and sets it as an example. "Behold, we count them happy which endure. Ye have heard of the patience of Job, and have seen the end of the Lord; that the Lord is very pitiful, and of tender mercy." (James 5:11.)

Rick Warren paints a misleading picture of Isaiah and Job and while passing by their powerful and "purpose driven" example of unflinching hope and courage, he quotes Dr. Bernie Siegel's experience, which in itself might seem harmless. Yet it is not only given in contrast to that of two of the greatest men of Scripture; but, more seriously, it offers a method that, instead of depending upon the Holy Spirit, depends upon the spirit which deceived Eve in Eden and will soon sweep the world into universal deception.

In June 1978, Dr. Bernie Siegel visited a workshop of the "Elmcrest Institute" in Portland, Connecticut, where he learned to meditate; and since that moment, George, a spirit Guide, in white garment, entered his life. Soon Siegel became a leading New Age teacher and writer. It is bizarre to note that Warren, with reference to hope and a purpose in life, decries unique biblical examples, such as Isaiah and Job, and mentions the experience of an active occult and spiritistic New Age leader. But Warren does not seem to have any problem with that. He freely quotes also other people with mystical, occultic, antichristian, and theosophical New Age idea's such as: Henri Nouwen, Madame Guyon, Aldous Huxley, Brennan Manning, Henry David Thoreau, Floyd McClung, George Bernard Shaw, and others.

The inexperienced may not realize it because it is rather inconspicuous, yet there's no doubt that Warren and his books do reflect New Age thinking, principles and teachings.

When former New Ager Warren Smith began reading *Purpose-Driven Life*, he was shocked to discover language, ideas, terms and philosophies that he learned in the New Age. With further research, Smith realized Purpose-Driven was indeed connected to the New Age, unbeknownst to thousands of well-intentioned believers. (*Deceived On Purpose,* Flyer, Lighthouse Trails Publishing, P.O. Box 958, Silverton, Oregon.)

Chapter 16

Prophecy

The prophecies in the Bible are a very important part of God's revelations to mankind and we should never ignore these sure words that provide light in darkness and certainty for the future. Warren, however, down plays the importance of prophecy. He writes in his book *The Purpose Driven Life*, on page 285:

> When the disciples wanted to talk about prophecy, Jesus quickly switched the conversation to evangelism. He wanted them to concentrate on their mission in the world. He said in essence, "The details of my return are none of your business. What **is** your business is the mission I've given you. Focus on that!"...If you want Jesus to come back sooner, focus on fulfilling your mission, not figuring out prophecy. It is easy to get distracted and sidetracked from your mission because Satan would rather have you do anything besides sharing your faith.

Prophecy is not merely very low on Warren's banner. He actively discourages study of the prophetic word because he considers this a snare of Satan to keep us from our mission.

Ellen White's following words could hardly be better tailored to Warren's efforts to defuse prophecy:

> Satan is not asleep; he is wide-awake to make of no effect the sure word of prophecy. With skill and deceptive power he is working to counterwork the expressed will of God, made plain in His word. (*Testimonies for the Church*, vol. 9, p. 92.)

> Every day adds its sorrowful evidence that faith in the sure word of prophecy is decreasing, and that in its stead superstition and

satanic witchery are captivating the minds of many. (*Prophets and Kings*, p. 210.)

Warren even dares to assert that Jesus made clear that the details of His coming are none of our business—we must focus on our mission—that is our business and not prophecy.

But is not prophecy a special part of our mission? Consider these words: "There are many who do not understand the prophecies relating to these days, and they must be enlightened." (*The Home Missionary*, p. 4.)

Explaining prophecy is a clear and necessary part of our mission to enlighten the people!

What about the coming of Christ and our mission? Are we not called to prepare ourselves and others for the soon return of Christ? And are the details of His coming not **absolutely indispensable** if we don't want to be misled? The **opposite** of what Warren wants to have us believe is true.

It is indeed Satan's plan to put all kinds of distractions in our path to keep us from heeding His sure word of prophecy, that we shall have no certainty and insight as into the things that befall us, so that he can easily mislead us. One who urges us to neglect prophecy and asserts that the details of our Lord's return are none of our business is an apt agent for Satan's plan. And since so many churches are following Warren's teachings, a great mass of people will be **unprepared** and **deceived** when Satan appears as "Christ" on earth.

Of this, Texe Marrs warns:

> The Plan of Satan, now being meticulously executed by his New Age followers, is to mimic the prophesied return of Jesus Christ. This will be Satan's boldest trick ever. His fake 'Messiah' will imitate the real Christ by performing miracles. His charismatic charm and perceived spiritual wisdom will so enchant world leaders and the masses that they will hail this 'Christ' as the greatest and most advanced man to have ever lived. Eventually almost every man, woman, and child in the world will worship him as God. New Age literature abounds with predictions about the imminent appearance of this false 'Christ.'...The New Age believes that its 'Messiah,' also called the Great World Teacher, will lead a One World Government and a One World Religion. (Texe Marrs, *Dark Secrets*

of the New Age, 1987, pp. 56, 57.)

Ellen White writes:

> As the crowning act in the great drama of deception, Satan himself will personate Christ. The church has long professed to look to the Saviour's advent as the consummation of her hopes. Now the great deceiver will make it appear that Christ has come. In different parts of the earth, Satan will manifest himself among men as a majestic being of dazzling brightness, resembling the description of the Son of God given by John in the Revelation (Revelation 1:13–15). The glory that surrounds him is unsurpassed by anything that mortal eyes have yet beheld. The shout of triumph rings out upon the air: "Christ has come! Christ has come!" The people prostrate themselves in adoration before him, while he lifts up his hands and pronounces a blessing upon them…Like the Samaritans who were deceived by Simon Magus, the multitudes, from the least to the greatest, give heed to these sorceries, saying: "This is 'the great power of God." Acts 8:10. (*The Great Controversy*, pp. 624, 625.)

How important are God's sure Word of Prophecy details of Christ's coming. What a tragedy that the modern church-growth leaders are down-playing the divine prophetic warnings and revelations concerning the time of the End. Can we believe that Jesus, instead of speaking with his disciples about prophecy, quickly switched the conversation to evangelism, as if prophecy is less important, as Warren suggests according to Acts 1:6–8?

What can we say about Christ's discussion with his disciples shortly before His death? Why did he give details and signs of His coming and of the end of the world and urge us not to be misled? He expects us to heed the prophetic words He spoke, and accordingly warned: "Take heed that no man deceive you." (Matthew 24:4)

But how can we do that if, as Warren asserts, the details are none of our business? How then can we recognize truth from error?

It is absolutely necessary to understand the prophecies and know beforehand the revealed details of Christ's coming to be prepared to meet the true Christ and not to be misled by a false Christ and false prophets. The word of prophecy is indispensable and invaluable to Christians who don't want to be deceived and who are called to serve as watchmen to warn and protect others

as well.

Jesus focused the attention of His disciples on Daniel the prophet: "When ye therefore shall see the abomination of desolation, spoken of by Daniel the prophet, stand in the holy place, whoso readeth let him understand." (Matthew 24:15.)

If Warren doesn't appreciate the sure word of prophecy; it must be clear that his teaching is not in accordance with Scripture for we read: "Despise not prophesyings." (1 Thess. 5:20)

We thus do well as we take heed to the prophecies. We are warned, "...there are some, also, who refuse to hear anything concerning the prophecies; the blessing is not for this class." (*The Great Controversy*, p. 341.)

If Warren says we should focus on our mission, rather than on prophecy, we can say that instead of receiving God's blessing he and all those who follow him in this way will at last find themselves in darkness, since they have no shining light. Concerning the light he rejects, the apostle Peter says,

> We have also a more sure word of prophecy; whereunto ye do well that ye take heed, as unto a light that shineth in a dark place... For the prophecy came not in old time by the will of man: but holy men of God spake as they were moved by the Holy Ghost. (2 Peter 1:19–21)

Prophecy is thus not the work of natural man, but of "holy men of God" who "were moved by the Holy Ghost."

Consider the following quote by Elwood McQuaid:

> Millions of grassroots Christians have developed a great hunger to understand what's going on today, where it's taking us, and what we should be doing about it. And these very concerns are the primary reason God gave us prophecies in the Bible. There is an abundance of evidence to substantiate the desire of many believers to be taught how to understand our present day and the future. Just ask pastors, evangelists, Bible teachers, or broadcasters who consistently present sound and sane prophetic truth in their ministries. They will tell you that they are constantly overwhelmed by inquiries and besieged by people requesting more information about the end times...There are ministers today who say that they have no personal position on the subject of Bible prophecy. To them, I suppose,

it seems outmoded, unintellectual, too complicated to tackle, or has no relevance to their ministry. But in neglecting prophecy, they are neglecting a full one-third of God's message to His people, which is a sad commentary on the inadequacy of their ministries. (Elwood McQuaid, *Persecuted, Exposing the Growing Intolerance Toward Christianity*, Harvest House Publ., Eugene, Oregon, 2003, p. 132, 133.)

Chapter 17

Immortality

The first lie introduced by the Devil into the Garden of Eden was the immortality of the human soul. Many church growth leaders believe in this unbiblical teaching. "Pastor Warren also firmly believes in the immortality of the human soul..." (Epinions.com, *Review Summary: The Purpose-Driven Life*, Paragraph 7, September 22, 2003.)

The natural immortality is the foundation of spiritism, by which millions of people are misled. We read: "But after the Fall, Satan bade his angels make a special effort to inculcate the belief in man's natural immortality..." (E. G. White, *The Great Controversy*, p. 534.)

If we proclaim the old mythological teaching of natural immortality, then, in fact, we back up Satan and his angels in their special effort.

Especially for the time of the end, certain great and important truths, including the immortality of the soul will protect against misleading dangers.

> The only safety now is to search for the truth as revealed in the word of God, as for hid treasure. The subjects of the Sabbath, the nature of man, and the testimony of Jesus, are the great and important truths to be understood; these will prove as an anchor to hold God's people in these perilous times. But the mass of mankind despise the truths of God's word, and prefer fables. (E. G. White, *Testimonies for the Church*, vol. 1, p. 300.)

Clear insight concerning the great and important truth about man's nature is essential. If we believe in the immortality of the soul, we miss a very important part of the anchor which gives us certainty and a firm hold in these perilous times.

Chapter 18

Lutheran Praesidium

The seriousness of the Church Growth Movement penetration is illustrated in the 1999 action of the Lutheran Praesidium and their later acknowledgement of inability to carry it out.

The general committee—the Praesidium—of the Lutheran Church of the Missouri Synod, under the leadership of its president, Dr. A. L. Barry, made an important decision in 1999 in response to complaints made against Doctor Robert Nordlie, Pastor of The Congregation of Redeemer Lutheran Church, Wayzata, Minnesota.

Pastor Nordlie was charged with teaching doctrine contrary to the fundamental principles of the gospel concerning righteousness, sanctification, law, and gospel obedience. Nordlie tried to justify himself, but the eventual judgment was that the serious concerns about his teachings were indeed well founded. The Praesidium concluded that the false teachings of Nordlie were responsible for the confusion and dismay in his congregation and abroad. The Praesidium desired that the Gospel of our Lord Jesus Christ would be taught and preached in a sound manner, so that under the blessing of God, the Holy Spirit could achieve a restoration of peace and unity in Christ. But they hoped Pastor Nordlie would be capable of acknowledging and correcting the shortcomings in his teaching and preaching.

Pastor Jack Cascione writes that Nordlie was found guilty but wasn't suspended from his pastorate. We read:

> There are so many pastors in the LCMS who are confused on the preaching of the Gospel promoted by the Church Growth Movement that the Praesidium will allow it to continue...Districts such as Michigan, Texas, Southern, Florida-Georgia, California-

Hawaii-Nevada, Pacific Southwest are so thoroughly infected with the Church Growth Movement that the Praesidium has come to the conclusion that it is now virtually impossible to maintain the correct teaching of the Gospel in the LCMS...

Cascione continues:

Nordlie's approach is just the kind of preaching necessary for Dr. Norbert Oesch of PLI, the COP, and LCEF to staff, build, and grow lots of "Willow Creek Community Churches" in the LCMS... Barry has chosen the course of peace, not to protect the Gospel but to protect the Synod from the Gospel...It is expedient that the Gospel be compromised so that the LCMS not perish...The irony is how well the Praesidium is doing its job. They did exceptional work in identifying and articulating Nordlie's theological error...Their assessment that Nordlie's error is shared by many other pastors in the Synod shows their clear understanding of its impact on the Synod. They are truthful and forthright in explaining the doctrinal errors. There is no cover-up here. They exhibit a heartfelt desire to confess the truth of the Gospel and make a good public confession to Jesus Christ. Then, beyond comprehension, with all this accumulated theological training, wisdom, experience, and discernment they publicly announce that for the good of the Synod they aren't going to do anything about it... The right teaching of the Gospel has become too heavy a cross for the LCMS. (*Reclaimnews*, 19/3, 1999, Internet. Center, 1333 South Kirkwood Rd., St. Louis, MO 63122-7295, paragraph break added.)

Many churches who follow God's Word and respect it, gradually got into trouble, because, without sufficient study, they opened their doors for the church-growth movement in an enthusiastic and trusting way.

November 1999, there were 25 theses written on the door of the church of the Richland Hills Church by concerned members and friends.

J. E. Choate writes:

I have read with heightened interest the 25 theses addressed to the Richland Church of Christ...The churches of Christ are again divided as wide as that gulf Jesus talked about. Once again there are multiple dividing lines which separate the churches, and the gulf keeps widening: These dividing lines are clearly marked:

POST MODERN THEOLOGY WHERE INSTRUMENTAL MUSIC, YOU NAME IT, AND IT GOES CHURCH GROWTH MODELS SUCH AS WILLOW CREEK; and others of the "theater of the weird and absurd, e.g., THE THIRD WAVE, KANSAS CITY PROPHETS, and the VINEYARD CHURCHES." (*Reply Concerned Members*, November 6, 2002. Emphasis in original.)

Chapter 19

Willow Creek Captures SDA Pastors

It's all the rage these days to follow the Alpha course, to study Rick Warren's books or to visit church-growth sessions at Willow Creek or other churches. We mislead ourselves as we become enchanted by the successes in churches where God has a controversy and go there to learn and apply their man-made methods. (Cf., EGW Comments Rev. 18:8) And the results of ignoring divine counsel regarding this have been very costly.

Says Ellen White: "Those who are studying the ways and methods of men and following their customs, are deceived if they think that they are following the directions of God in the matter." (*The Signs of the Times,* August 27, 1894, p. 660.)

The very things Ellen White described are happening before our eyes today in the modern church-growth movement:

> Ministers of popular churches are many of them softening down and diluting the plain word of truth. They are obscuring the light, and changing the message, in order to accomodate it to the prejudices, and adjust it to the opinions and habits, of the people. Thus they cater to the taste of the world-loving members of the church. (Ibid., p. 659.)

A dozen years earlier Ellen White warned: "Some ministers are adopting the customs of other churches, copying their habits and manner of labor." (Ibid., May 25, 1882, p. 236.)

What are the results in our days as our ministers adopt customs and copy habits and manner of labor of other churches?

Gregory E. Taylor, an SDA pastor, visited Willow Creek with his wife several times to attend training-sessions. Gradually they became impressed by the atmosphere, the principles and methods applied there and soon **doubts** about their own religious conviction **arose** which caused a close self-examination.

Carl F. George, a non-Adventist church-growth specialist at Fuller Theological Seminary, visited about this time a colleague to help supervise and to advise concerning church-growth. Gregory writes:

> Carl George's assessment was that they could not break into the unchurched community because of the Sabbath issues. This was too great a barrier for most people not brought up or married into Adventism.

Soon they gave up the Sabbath and held services on Sunday.

As some other Adventist pastors were also struggling with the Sabbath, Gregory started an intense study on this issue. He was amazed to view the New Testament presentation of the Sabbath in a different way than he always had believed.

He testifies:

> We have come to an understanding of the Bible in a whole new and powerful way...I learned...that the Sabbath was an institution that pointed forward to Jesus and therefore was no longer binding on Christians...All I can say is that I have seen a picture of God and His word that has shattered all my previous paradigms. I am grateful for this gift of God's grace. (G. E. Taylor, *An open letter to our Friends and Family. Truth or Fables*, April 6, 2003.)

Here we clearly see the very "paradigm shift" so fervently proclaimed in the church-growth movement and in the New Age, as a necessity that must take place.

In personal correspondence, Gregory confirmed that Willow Creek has had a great influence on his way of thinking and on his decision to leave the SDA church. He also confirmed that others followed a similar path.

He writes:

> Yes, one of the men I was studying with has taken his church out of the SDA system into an evangelical church. There are others.

Clay Peck in Berthoud, Colorado, Richard Fredericks in Damascus, Maryland, and I have heard of others. (*Correspondence with G. E. Taylor*, Nov. 9 and 18, 2004.)

Listen to Clay Peck's testimony, which reveals how in visiting Willow Creek many times he was caught and turned away from Adventism by the principles of the modern church-growth experts:

> It became a hobby of mine to read and learn about various principles for growth that were being advocated by church growth experts...Shortly after seminary I visited Willow Creek Community Church in Chicago. Since then I've been back many times. God is doing an awesome work there...I wondered how that could be 'Babylon' and how I could call people out of that into what Adventism had to offer. This created more cognitive dissonance for me. For a number of years I went through a gradual Grace Awakening...As a pastor in Davenport IA, while I was still doing Prophecy Crusades, I began to try and weave the gospel of grace in more and more. (*My Journey Out of Legalism*, pp. 5, 6.)

As Clay Peck visited Willow Creek he became convinced that **God is doing an awesome work there** and his vision about Adventism diminished. He claims to have focused more and more on the gospel of grace rather than on the obligation of God's Law, which ultimately led him to abandon the sabbath. But what he really studied was the Willow Creek counterfeit of grace.

If he had truly focused more and more upon grace he would have seen the intimate bond between grace and law and have radiated our doctrine of judgment, Sabbath, etc., with the grace which gives them life and meaning. Nowhere can you find a more intense bonding of grace and law than in Ellen White's writings. Not only in books such as *Steps to Christ* and *The Desire of Ages,* but in such books as *Patriarch's and Prophets* and even *The Great Controversy.* Grace represents God's love. And His law is a transcript of His love.

Ellen White, speaking of the glorious preparation of a people for the Lord's second coming, warns that Satan will hinder this mighty work of the Spirit presenting beforehand a counterfeit:

> In those churches which he can bring under his deceptive power he will make it appear that God's special blessing is poured out;

there will be manifest what is thought to be great religious interest. **Multitudes will exult that God is working marvelously** for them, when the work is that of another spirit. (*The Great Controversy,* p. 464, emphasis added.)

We are also given the secret of how to discern the lack of the Spirit and power of God in the end time revivals:

> The nature and the importance of the law of God have been, to a great extent, lost sight of. A wrong conception of the character, the perpetuity, and the obligation of the divine law has led to errors in relation to conversion and sanctification, and has resulted in lowering the standard of piety in the church. Here is to be found the secret of the lack of the Spirit and power of God in the revivals of our time. (Ibid., p. 465.)

Consider, for instance, how God's law is arbitrarily interpreted by the Willow Creek Pastors in a way to deny the holiness of the Sabbath:

> Often our Pastors have applied the command to 'rest' to moments of reflection in nature and quiet moments with God whenever they happen... The observance of Time is no longer sufficient to satisfy what the Sabbath is all about. (Richard Hirst, Willow Creek Pastor answers question about 7th day sabbath, October 21, 2003.)

The sabbath command of God's holy appointed time for man is thus made subordinate to our desires and tailored to what suits us best. But to deny that the observance of time is no longer binding is to repudiate the unabated perpetuity and obligation of the divine law.

Note also other features Ellen White describes about counterfeit revivals that precisely fit the modern church-growth movement:

> There is an emotional excitement, a mingling of the true with the false, that is well adapted to mislead...Wherever men neglect the testimony of the Bible, turning away from those plain, soul testing truths which require self-denial and renunciation of the world, there we may be sure that God's blessing is not bestowed. (Ibid., p. 464.)

> The hope of salvation is accepted without a radical change of heart or reformation of life. Thus superficial conversions abound, and multitudes are joined to the church who have never been united

to Christ. Erroneous theories of sanctification, also, springing from neglect or rejection of the divine law, have a prominent place in the religious movements of the day. (Ibid., pp. 468, 469.)

The sanctification now gaining prominence in the religious world carries with it a spirit of self-exaltation and a disregard for the law of God that mark it as foreign to the religion of the Bible. Its advocates teach that sanctification is an instantaneous work, by which, through faith alone, they attain to perfect holiness. "Only believe," say they, "and the blessing is yours." (Ibid., p. 471.)

In summarizing the religion of the church-growth movement, Clay Millar declared at the 2003 Shepherds' Conference, that they presume to save people without teaching them,

...the great doctrines of the Christian faith—Justification, Sanctification. Don't use words like that—you'll scare people away!

Miller continues:

In short, people are not saved...by the Word of God in this system...I would say that the church growth movement misunderstands and strikes a blow at the doctrine of sanctification.

He declares that the church growth movement,

...strikes a blow at almost every major doctrine: depravity, election, regeneration, sanctification, worship and even evangelism. The sad reality is that this movement, which began with the intent and the motive to evangelize the lost, I would say emasculates true evangelism...I would say this, that, without clear, solid, heavily studied, expository preaching, at mining and exposing the deep truths that God has revealed in His word—that will produce a barren wasteland of doctrine. And that barren wasteland of doctrine will produce a barren wasteland of truth, which will produce a barren wasteland of believers which means churches, sadly filled with unbelievers—thinking they are believers—coming and worshipping a God that they don't even know. (*Church Growth Gone Mad, A sobering look at the church growth seeker-sensitive models,* Outreach Ministries, 2003.)

It is no surprise that meanwhile, the influence of mega-churches, such as Willow Creek and Saddleback, has not enabled us to proclaim our specific God-given time of the end message more successfully. Nor has it helped us to gain a higher and better spiritual level. Indeed, the opposite is clearly true!

> Several Sabbath-keeping congregations have adopted the church growth methods used by the popular Willow Creek and other non traditional churches. The results are undeniable…One administrator lamented the huge amounts of money, which have been lost on such church plants with poor returns There has been an incredible loss of finances, churches, pastors, and worse, souls in Sabbath-keeping churches when rock music and drum sets are used. (Karl Tsatalbasidis, *Drums, Rock, and Worship, Amazing Facts*, 2003, p. 55, 57.)

Ellen White writes:

> Yielding to Satan's sophistry, they stand on a false track, and by their representations endeavor to tear down truths that God has made fast, never to be moved…When brought into strait places, they will give up the Sabbath and its powerful endorsement, and the more they are opposed in their apostasy, the more self-sufficient and self-deceived they become. (*Manuscript Releases*, vol. 10, pp. 46, 47.)

Chapter 20

A Firm Stand

If we believe we have a God given commission to proclaim the last message of mercy to the world and all the churches, how credible will that be when we go to them for advice and instruction on how to be successful, as if we are short of God's guidance in reaching people with His message. We need to take a firm stand without any compromise with worldly men.

Ellen White speaks to the point:

> There is to be no compromise with those who make void the law of God. It is not safe to rely upon them as counselors. Our testimony is not to be less decided now than formerly; our real position is not to be cloaked in order to please the world's great men. They may desire us to unite with them and accept their plans, and may make propositions in regard to our course of action which may give the enemy an advantage over us. (*Selected Messages,* book two, p. 371.)

How true these words are!

Note Ezra's firm stand:

> Ezra and his companions had determined to fear and obey God, and to put their trust wholly in Him. They would not form a connection with the world in order to secure the help or friendship of the enemies of God. Whether they were with the many or the few, they knew that success could come from God only. And they had no desire that their success should be attributed to the wealth or influence of wicked men. (Ellen G. White Comments, *Bible Commentary,* vol., 3, p. 1134.)

The success of God's Church today should not be attributed to the influence of man-made methods. Just as God was with Ezra and his companions, so He will be with His church today. It is true that there are technical innovations, especially in areas such as radio, TV, and email which provide new avenues of proclaiming the gospel. We can't honestly claim to have developed the ultimate in these avenues and other modern methods of presentation. But God has given us clear principles and every new method explored must be tested by those principles. And as we do, the glory goes to Him, who guards His church with jealous care. Nothing else in this world is so dear to God as His church. Nothing is guarded by Him with such jealous care." (*Testimonies for the Church,* Vol., 6, p. 42.)

Ellen White repeats this thought several times: "Nothing in this world is so dear to the heart of God as His church. It is not His will that worldly policy shall corrupt her record." (*Prophets and Kings,* p. 590.)

Do we really believe these words?

If God guards His church "with jealous care" could we then regard her destitute and insufficient somehow? Is there really any need then to learn elsewhere methods and strategies that should secure success?

We are encouraged with a wonderful promise and assurance of success in church growth:

> Nothing else in this world is so dear to God as His church. He will work with mighty power through humble, faithful men. Christ is saying to you to-day: "I am with you, co-operating with your faithful, trusting efforts, and giving you precious victories. I will strengthen you as you sanctify yourselves to My service. **I will give you success in your efforts to arouse souls dead in trespasses and sins.**" (Ibid., vol. 7, pp. 242, 243. Emphasis added.)

Note that God "will work with **mighty power** through **humble** and **faithful** men"! Those seeking to develop modern mega-churches are in danger of cultivating pride and developing worldly methods. But if we look to Him for counsel, He promises to **co-operate in giving victories**! This is our great need. He will give **success** in our ministry **to arouse dead souls!** Isn't that **real** church growth?

When we are assured of mighty power—assured of divine cooperation in gaining victories—assured of success in arousing dead souls to life; why then do we need to go to other churches for instruction how to be successful in church growth? Could it be that we ourselves need to be aroused because we are not claiming that power?

Is it not an act of unbelief and an insult to God when, with all these precious unfailing divine promises, we go instead to the sources of this world which deliberately discourage a focus upon truth? Rather, should we not prayerfully study God's principles and seek divine help to be humble and faithful while firmly claiming God's promises?

Listen to the prophet Jeremiah:

> For my people have committed two evils; they have forsaken me the fountain of living waters, and hewed them out cisterns, broken cisterns, that can hold no water…And now what hast thou to do in the way of Egypt, to drink the waters of Sihor? or what hast thou to do in the way of Assyria, to drink the waters of the river? (Jer. 2:13, 18.)

God has called us as His people with a special message. We are assured of His power and encouraged by His wonderful promises. In view of this, are we not repeating the two-fold evil of ancient Israel when we go to these other sources for advice and instruction?

God, in His jealous care, has given us so much advice and instruction through His messenger, Ellen White. Were her messages appropriate in her days but now outdated? Could we assert that she had no notion of the modern age we now live in? If we accept that she was inspired by God, can we then believe when God gave her His messages, He had no notion of the present modern age? Should we not rather trust God's omniscience and venture in faith upon His wisdom?

We may be assured that modern methods may develop but divine principles never change. Violation of those principles is our great danger today. God's church will truly grow and be blessed when we take a firm stand on our God given principles and instruction and humbly and faithfully claim His wonderful promises.

Chapter 21

Sincere Conversion

In order to be saved and live an obedient and devout life, according to the will of God, the sinner must be set free of every kind of self-confidence and self-esteem, surrendering himself to the power of God's Spirit to be revived to a completely new life.

This fundamental message must not be ignored simply because it is not in accordance with the modern marketing techniques or the "felt needs" method recommended for church-growth. Neither must this message be replaced by a mixture of Pelagian-Arminian teachings or psychological and philosophical insights of occult origin, nor by the charismatic and ecumenical ideas of the New Age movement!

Although it seems that little attention is given, yet we can be grateful for the warning voices that are heard. Note how Clay Miller warns against the "felt needs" method to win people genuinely for Christ:

> Here a quote from Rick Warren, "It is my deep conviction that anybody can be won to Christ if you discover the key to his or her heart, and the most likely place to start looking for that key is within the person's felt needs." This is man centered Arminianism! It fails to recognize that a pagan's felt needs spring from the soil of a dark, stony, unregenerate heart. We shouldn't care one bit about someone's felt needs. We don't need a survey to determine a pagan's felt needs… A pagan's felt needs are comfort, sex, money and recognition—there you go, you don't need a survey. And what we care about is the true need which is reconciliation to God. That's what we care about, that's the need that we care about. (*Church Growth Gone Mad, A sobering look at the church growth seeker-sensitive models,* Outreach Ministries, Shepherds' Conference, 2003.)

Here is another warning voice:

> The philosophy that marries marketing technique with church growth theory is the result of bad theology. It assumes that if you package the gospel right, people will get saved. It is rooted in Arminianism, which views conversion as nothing more than an act of the human will. Its goal is an instantaneous human decision, rather than a radical transformation of the heart wrought by almighty God through the Holy Spirit's convicting work and the truth of His Word. An honest belief in the sovereignty of God in salvation would bring an end to a lot of the nonsense that is going on in the church. (John MacArthur, *But Does It Work? Truth Vs. Technique. Good Technique? No, Bad Theology.*)

MacArthur is correct in discerning the problem and recognizes the dangers of the Arminian imbalance. Unfortunately, he does not recognize that his own Calvinistic, pre-destinarian views have also contributed to the confusion which has permitted such a sinister development.

Did Jesus apply marketing techniques in his ministry on earth to win souls? It is obvious that Jesus didn't speak to amuse people. He didn't adapt His gospel to please the people or to pleasantly entertain them. When a great multitude was gathered around Him, He spoke to them the Word of Truth in a **clear** and **plain** manner and many said: "This is an hard saying; who can hear it?" We even read: "From that time many of his disciples went back, and walked no more with him."

According to modern ideas, Jesus had almost founded a mega-church, but now many went back and walked no more with Him. Why didn't Jesus present His message in a nicer, friendlier way? Why such a hard and hurting message? Could He have learned a lot from the current church-growth specialists? Or do they, with their comfortable and satisfying way of preaching, have much to learn of Christ? Notice that we don't even read that Jesus tried to bring the people back to Him. No, He merely asked the twelve disciples if they too would leave Him. Indeed, Jesus pointed out a fundamental reality greatly needed by engineers of market-driven conversions, but which they carefully avoid. Jesus said: "No man can come unto me, except it were given unto him of my Father." (John. 6:60–67)

Jesus knew that all who followed Him with selfish motives would soon be an offence to His work. A great number of people who profess to follow Him, now as in His day, are not truly converted and connected with the true vine. Their faith is not sincere and the test will reveal their weak and unreliable character. They're not as Christ expects them to be: meek and lowly of heart, self-denying, self-sacrificing, and walking on the narrow path where Jesus went before them as the Man of Sorrows. Just as in His day, for many the test will be too heavy. They will find the words of Jesus too hard to hear and will ultimately turn away from Him and no longer follow Him.

Ellen White wrote:

> When truth is brought home to the heart, they see that their lives are not in accordance with the will of God. They see the need of an entire change in themselves; but they are not willing to take up the self-denying work. Therefore they are angry when their sins are discovered. They go away offended, even as the disciples left Jesus, murmuring, 'This is an hard saying; who can hear it?' Praise and flattery would be pleasing to their ears; but the truth is unwelcome; they cannot hear it. When the crowds follow, and the multitudes are fed, and the shouts of triumph are heard, their voices are loud in praise; but when the searching of God's Spirit reveals their sin, and bids them leave it, they turn their backs upon the truth, and walk no more with Jesus. (E. G. White, *The Desire of Ages*, p. 392.)

Christ clearly placed the message of truth central and aimed at true conversion for all His followers. He brought the truth in a kind but outspoken way, even if it was hard to hear.

By contrast, George Barna, a leading church-growth strategist who cooperates with Bill Hybels of Willow Creek and with the Saddleback Church of Rick Warren, says:

It is...critical that we keep in mind a fundamental principle of Christian communication: the audience, not the message, is sovereign...our message has to be adapted to the needs of the audience. (George Barna, *Marketing the Church*, Colorado Springs: NavPress, 1988, p 145.)

We should follow the example of Christ. Circumstances may call for a change in approach, but never in underlying principle or in the message!

We are called to be faithful servants of a great and reliable Biblical inheritance. We must proclaim and defend a great mes-

sage. And this means we must discern and avoid error.
We are not to weaken the truth in order to please people and make it more attractive and appealing to them that way. (Cf., Heidinger, *'Toxic Pluralism' Christianity Today*, April 5, 1993, p. 16, 17.)

Chapter 22

Commercial Methods

In *Business Week*, European Edition, May 23, 2005, Rick Warren's book *The Purpose Driven Life* is called: a *Marketing Miracle*. "Rick Warren used an innovative tactic called 'pyro marketing'..." (p. 56.)

The Cover Story of this Business Magazine is: "*Evangelical America—Big Business—Explosive Politics.*"

On page 2 we read:

> Marketing Masters. How evangelical churches employ a panoply of business techniques to pull in new members... Evangelical entrepreneurs are transforming their branch of Protestantism into the fastest-growing and most influential religious cohort in the U.S. Using tools ranging from focus groups to brand management, they're borrowing from business to boost their market share of American churchgoers.

And on pages 48-56 we find a special report on

> Earthly Empires, How evangelical churches are borrowing from the business playbook...Managing the Mega Church, A new class of entrepreneurial evangelicals is using commercial methods to win new members...Evangelicals are launching new mega churches... using mass-marketing tactics...and gaining market share...making them the largest force in U.S. religion. (pp. 50, 51.)

The role of the mega-churches is not only religious and commercial, but also political. We read: "Evangelical's influence in American political life has become increasingly visible in recent years." (p. 54.)

Willow Creek founder Bill Hybels...hired Stanford MBA Greg Hawkins, a former McKinsey & Co. consultant, to handle the church's day-to-day management. Willow Creek's methods have even been lauded in a Harvest Business School case study. (p. 55.)

Willow Creek has a budget of $48 million and $143 million in net assets. (p. 52.) "Willow Creek ranks in the top 5% of 250 major brands, right up with Nike and John Deere…" (p. 56.) "Hybel's consumer-driven approach is evident at Willow Creek, where he shunned stained glass, Bibles, or even a cross for the 7,200-seat, $72 million sanctuary he recently built." (p. 55.)

That beautiful and expensive 72 million dollar building, provided with the latest technical novelties, is very impressive. And what's more, the "message" is brought in a contemporary way with modern Christian pop-music, drama, multimedia, and all kinds of adapted interesting social themes.

But has this still anything to do with the powerful simplicity of the truth of the Gospel message by which one has to be drawn?

It appears that the message of the Bible and the reverential and dedicated church service is being exchanged for a general social event. This happening, instead of being a solemn service, looks more like an attractive entertainment show to amuse and satisfy the people in a lucrative way to hold them together.

Note Ellen White's words in this context:

> A religion which seeks only to gratify the eye, the ear, and the taste, or which permits any hurtful self-indulgence, is not the religion of Christ. It is in harmony with the spirit of the world, and is opposed to the teachings of the Holy Scriptures. Festivals and scenes of amusement, in which professed members of the Christian church imitate the customs and enjoy the pleasures of the world, constitute a virtual union with the enemies of God. (E. G. White, *Sketches from the Life of Paul*, p. 170.)

Chapter 23

Total Quality Management

Rick Warren of Saddleback church, as well as Bill Hybels of the Willow Creek community have both been educated in marketing methodology by Peter Drucker and Bob Buford, his follower. Warren says: "I read everything Peter Drucker writes. His book *'The Effective Executive'* is a favourite I re-read every year." (Rick Warren, *Building on Your Strengths.*)

Robert Schuller asserts that he was the one who introduced the marketing approach in the church:

> An undisputed historical fact is that I am the founder, really, of the church-growth movement in this country...I advocated and launched what has become known as the marketing approach in Christianity. (G. A. Pritchard, *Willow Creek Seeker Services*, Baker Books, 1998, p. 51.)

Worldly marketing techniques do not agree with Christ's declaration that His Kingdom is not of this world. And it is sad to state that besides the improper influence of Robert Schuller, who is a New Age follower and 33rd degree Freemason, the tie with management and marketing expert Peter Drucker has granted dubious impetus to the modern church-growth movement. How are we to assess this unbecoming influence?

Peter Drucker (1909–2005), an Austrian, together with the late Edwards Deming, are generally regarded as well known international experts in business management. The philosophy and methodology of both these men were particularly successful in Japan after the destructions of the Second World War. In the west, Drucker experienced initial resistance against his ideas which in the core, are not original, but came from the ranks of the 19th Century esoteric Germanic philosophy. Drucker's concepts of his "Management by Objective" and "Total Quality Management" (TQM), can be traced back to the teachings of Hegel, Marx, Nietzsche, Wellhausen, Blavatsky, and others and are in line with the insights of the New Age. The system of Drucker's TQM has a clear esoteric undercurrent. This met with initial resistance. However, in Japan, where the esoteric mysteries of eastern religions are common, it was accepted very favourably. After a successful period in Japan, General Motors was the first company to open its doors to Drucker's management system. Once the first doors were opened, the floodgates burst. Before long it seemed that everyone was saturated with this methodology and even the church-growth leaders opened their doors to this worldly philosophical business system.

Notice what David M. Boje and Robert D. Windsor wrote about Drucker's TQM:

> The thesis of this article is that as an economic phenomenon, total quality management has been positioned as a carefully engineered set of technological process modifications which purport to lead to enhanced levels of product quality or lower costs and thereby provide the ability to achieve and sustain a global competitive advantage. To achieve these spoils, however, TQM directly and covertly alters the values, culture, and mind-sets within an organization. As a result, and parallel to these technological modifications, TQM establishes a carefully integrated programme of social and psychological engineering which is critical to the 'successful' implementation of TQM and which has a significant impact on the behaviour and consciousness of both managers and workers. (*'The Resurrection of Taylorism: Total Quality Management's Hidden Agenda,'* The Journal of Organisational Change Management, Vol. 6, 1993, p. 57.)

This is not without danger. TQM directly and covertly alters the values, culture, and mindset and there is a significant impact on the behaviour and consciousness of both managers and workers. This system touches man's body, soul and spirit.

TQM seeks to perform control systems that produce and enforce uniformity within the products, parts, workers, suppliers, and the overall system of production. The problem is that a majority of this control, in line with Taylor's (1911) principles, is directed toward workers' bodies, souls, and spirits. (Ibid., p. 59.)

Mac Dominick writes in his manuscript:

> This aspect of the Drucker/Deming methodology seeks the same results—a paradigm shift—a change of mind from the old to the new, from the past to the future, from individualism to group dynamics, and from nationalism to globalism...the esoteric side of this issue comes to the fore when one begins to direct management principles toward the worker's body, soul, and spirit. This methodology crosses a threshold from the secular to the religious; and once one delves into religious arenas with humanistic methodology, the situation quickly transitions from mundane to esoteric levels. (Mac Dominick, *Outcome-Based Religion: Purpose, Apostasy, & The New Paradigm Church,* Cutting Edge Ministries, 2005, p. 293.)

The church-growth leaders brought the principles of this system into the church. Some aspects of this shift, we find, for instance, in Warren's book *The Purpose Driven Life*. A few headings in chapter 38 are: "Becoming a World-Class Christian" "How to Think Like a World-Class Christian" "Shift from local thinking to global thinking" "Shift from 'here and now' thinking to eternal thinking" "Shift from thinking of excuses to thinking of creative ways to fulfill your commission."

It is no accident that the church-growth leaders present this globalistic "paradigm shift" of thinking, that is in harmony with Drucker's methodology and with the New Age movement, as a central spearhead on the way to the One World Church.

Many of these objectives appear to be definitely in line with Christian principles. But heresy always involves "the tree of knowledge of good and evil." Among other problems two stand out. First, that truth is subordinated to unity in an "ends justify the means." Second, the methods of manipulation and coersion are classic evidences of Satanic direction, which the all powerful God has for 6,000 years refused to use and strictly forbids. This will become increasingly evident as we consider Rick Warren's "Shape-program" and the section on "New Age."

Chapter 24

Shape

In line with Peter Drucker's system is Rick Warren's "Shape-program" which will help you to determine your personality profile; to discover your purpose in your life and to find out how you can function more successfully in your life and perform your "ministry" or service for God more effectively. The "Shape-concept" is discussed in *The Purpose Driven Life* in the chapters 29 to 33. However, there is more to it that is not mentioned in the book.

Every prospective member is required to fill out the SHAPE questionnaire which contains several dubious aspects.

The application and understanding of your "shape" is a very important part of Warren's program and as for the information in the book, on a first quick look, one may be tempted to conclude that it is all presented in a nice biblical way. However, if we study all aspects carefully, we will find many unbiblical aspects and clear similarities with the ideas and concepts of Galen and Jung. There are several comparative studies and charts that bear this out.

In *The Sacred Sandwich* we find the following comments regarding this:

> Clearly, the fourth tenet of Warren's SHAPE program, the personality assessment test, is fully rooted in the pagan philosophy of temperament divination. It has no foundation whatsoever in any biblical teaching...

> At the risk of mixing metaphors, the SHAPE program is like a building constructed upon both rock and sand...Rick Warren, whether he realizes it or not, has utilized pagan and occult-

influenced psychological theory to help formulate the Personality Theory section of his SHAPE program...Whether Warren devotees want to admit it or not, Warren's SHAPE program for personality classification is directly tied to Galen's (and Jung's) pagan teachings on temperament and psychological typology. The facts clearly show that Warren has compromised his Christian beliefs with the ways of the pagan world. *(The Sacred Sandwich*, August 01, 2005, *The Pagan Roots of Rick Warren's Personality SHAPE.* p. 2, 3.)

If Warren did shape his Shape-program under the inspiration of Carl Jung's analytical ideas, how should we as Christians, relate to that? To unequivocally answer that question we need to consider the nature of Warren's resemblance to Jung and the source of Jung's psycho-philosophical concepts. A brief overview of Jung's history quickly dispels any idea that he and his teaching is in harmony with a living Christian faith, as based firmly upon the Word of God.

Carl Jung was born in 1875 at Basel and became a famous psychiatrist who formulated a system of analytical psychology. His friend Richard Wilhelm introduced the meaning of eastern wisdom and philosophy to him, to wit from China, India and Tibet. (*Christelijke Encyclopedie*, Kok, Kampen, dl. 4, p. 128.)

Carl Jung's family shows clear occult ties, while Carl was always very interested in paranormal phenomena, astrology and in calculating horoscopes. He was chiefly interested in the particular light the horoscope sheds on certain complications in the character and in cases of difficult psychological diagnosis, he usually took a horoscope. Carl also attended spiritualistic séances with his cousin Helene Preiswerk and he wrote his dissertation on her psychic experiences, *On Psychology and Pathology of So-Called Occult Phenomena* (1902).

> Beginning in 1913 he conversed with spirit guides, in particular a guide named Philemon, whom he called his "guru." One afternoon in the summer of 1916 Jung experienced spirits in his house. They gave him what was to be the first sentence, and under inspiration he wrote *Seven Sermons to the Dead* in three evenings. Jung felt that he was expressing the ideas of Philemon. (*The Charts: Pagan and Jungian Roots in Rick Warren's SHAPE Personality Testing*, p. 3.)

Jung was waging war against Christianity and its distant, absolute, unreachable God and was training his disciples to listen to the voice of the dead and to become gods themselves. (Richard Noll, *The Jung Cult*, p. 224.)

Carl Jung's influence, even in churches, is still very great. Jung is often described as "the psychologist of the 21st century." Dr. Satinover writes:

> Because of his great influence in propagating gnostic philosophy and morals in churches & synagogues, Jung deserves a closer look. The moral relativism that released upon us the sexual revolution is rooted in an outlook of which (Jung) is the most brilliant contemporary expositor. (Dr. Jeffrey Satinover, *Homosexuality and the Politics of Truth*, 1996, p. 238.)

Ed Hird says: "One could say without overstatement that Carl Jung is the Father of Neo-Gnosticism & the New Age Movement." Several views and aspects within the modern churches are directly related to Carl Jung's teachings. "Carl Jung is indeed the Grandfather of much of our current theology." (Anglican Renewal Ministries of Canada, *Carl Jung, Neo-Gnosticism, & The MBTI*, A report by Ed Hird, March 18, 1998, p. 4.)

Since Warren's "Shape-program" at its base, is in harmony with Jung's ideas, it is understandable that sincere Bible Christians do have problems with that.

A dangerous aspect is that when we once accept philosophical and mythological ideas and concepts which are unchristian in origin, it will then not be easy to be get free from it, for the enchanting, mysterious, and crafty powers, who inspired these concepts, will clearly reveal their tenacious influence.

If people once have chosen in favour of such teachings, then they will run the risk of receiving "strong delusion, that they should believe a lie." (2 Thess. 2:11)

James Sundquist, who in several chapters discussed Warren's Shape-program and uncovered many unbiblical aspects and philosophical unchristian New Age influences in Warren's book, writes:

> But you may be even more surprised to learn that even after clearly documenting a host of his false translations, false teachings,

and the false teachers he promotes, that even then these pastors would still try to defend him and simply refuse correction. (*Who's Driving the Purpose Driven Church? A Documantary on the Teachings of Rick Warren,* 2004, p. 189.)

Chris Carmichael, in his comparative study, demonstrates that Warren's shape-model is not only in harmony with Carl Jung's teachings but also in accordance with the ideas of Galen, a Greek philosopher and physician born in A.D. 131. Galen's hometown was Pergamum, the renowned site of heathen worship and center of many pagan cults. Pergamum was called the abode of "Satan's throne." (Rev. 2:13)

For any Christian who defends Warren's approach and sees no harm in applying Greek or Jungian psychological typology to their lives, you should be informed of the blatant pagan origins of these manmade theories Not all "truth" is God's truth, despite the prevalent sentiment of evangelical circles to profess such an idea. Just as Paul wisely resisted the temptation to apply Greek philosophy to the Christian faith in his day, so, too, should contemporary Christian leaders be wary of using the world's "wisdom" as a proper tool to build up the body of Christ. As Paul taught us, "Do not be unequally yoked with unbelievers." (*The Sacred Sandwich, The Purpose Driven Lie: Pagan Roots in Rick Warren's SHAPE Personality Testing,* p. 3, 4.)

Paganism, particularly, found its birth in Egypt and Babylon through the development of astrology and other man-made philosophies. As time passed, astrology spread to Persia and places beyond, and was eventually embraced by the Greeks who moulded astrology more in harmony with their philosophy and religion. Much of the philosophical aspects of historic astrology were used to create the Greek sciences that pertained to the body and soul, like psychology, anatomy and pharmacology.

On this basis with pagan-astrological leanings, Galen of Pergamum developed his ideas on the four temperaments, or humors, to study and understand the construct of the body and soul. Warren makes use of these temperaments in his personality program.

Galen based his beliefs on the earlier work of Empedocles and Hippocrates. Empedocles believed the universe was made up of four elements: fire, air, earth and water, with each having its own god or goddess. Hippocrates, known as the Father of Medicine, believed that these four elements had four corresponding body fluids or "humors." These were defined as blood, yellow bile, black bile, and phlegm; each one designating personality types. Galen took this premise and further developed the temperament theory into the four categories of melancholic, phlegmatic, sanguine, and choleric. (Ibid., p. 3.)

Galen's unchristian "temperament-theory" in fact is part of Warren's teaching about personality assessment in serving God. Thus, Warren, for example, even precisely tells us that, "Peter was a sanguine. Paul was a choleric. Jeremiah was a melancholy." (*The Purpose Driven Life,* p. 245.)

But this theory has no foundation in the Scriptures, but in fact finds its origin in Greek astrological, philosophical and mythological thinking. Thus one may run the risk of getting entangled in the snares of the enemy.

The Shape-program is much stressed as a valuable, unique, and indispensable tool to find out your gifts, abilities, personality, and your particular service for God.

SHAPE states:

> To discover your S.H.A.P.E. is to discover where God is calling you to do His work in the world. (James Sundquist, *Who's Driving the Purpose Driven Church?* Rock Salt Publ., 2004, p. 141.)

> You have now completed the S.H.A.P.E. Discovery Workshop. You have explored how God has SHAPE'd you for ministry through your spiritual gifts, heart, abilities, personality, and experience. (Ibid., p. 139.)

How enlightened, blessed and privileged are we in this modern 21st Century with this SHAPE Discovery Workshop. But are we really?

> The Church was not deficient for nineteen hundred years because it did not possess the secret knowledge and keys to one's personality and diagnostic tools through the SHAPE test. All of the martyred and persecuted saints throughout the ages had everything

they needed to be fully equipped to do the work of the ministry, including the ability to figure out what gift of the Holy Spirit they had. This whole idea is a reproach to every saint that ever lived and an insult to the sufficiency of Christ. (Ibid., p. 136.)

The martyred and persecuted saints throughout the ages are without doubt a very unique and humiliating example for today's self-conceited and self-satisfied men.

By fidelity and faith in Christ, they earned spotless robes and jewelled crowns. Their lives were ennobled and elevated in the sight of God, because they stood firmly for the truth under the most aggravated circumstances. (E. G. White, *Testimonies for the Church*, Vol. 4, p. 336.)

Notice further what SHAPE states:

Using the results of the Spiritual Gifts Assessment questionnaire on the following pages, list your top three Spiritual Gifts...

Assess your gifts matching the letter at the bottom of the row with the Spiritual Gift Assessment Key. (Sundquist, op. cit., p. 132.)

Consider this! Must we depend on a man-made and invented test sheet questionnaire to determine our top three Spiritual Gifts making use of a Spiritual Gift Assessment Key? Are we to determine our Gift(s) of the Spirit by adding up a score? Can we harmonize that somehow with the Bible? Are we ourselves, by our own will, to find out and decide upon the Gifts? Or is the Holy Spirit Who gives them committed to reveal what they are and how He would have us use them? The Bible says: "But all these worketh that one and the selfsame Spirit, dividing to every man severally as he will." (1 Cor. 12:11.)

The one and the same Spirit divides the Gifts as He will. And He is sent to guide us into all truth, not only of Scripture but of His purpose for us individually in giving us His gifts. (John 16:13; Isa 58:11) And He does this without a Shape profiling test, cunningly devised by man. Nor does He need a Spiritual Gift Assessment Key.

You are asked to list your top three Spiritual Gifts, but what if the Spirit has given you only two or perhaps just one? Are you then going to invent one or two Gifts as you think might suit you? A more serious

issue is the purpose of SHAPE to develop a pattern of dependence upon its authors rather than upon a personal relation with God through His Spirit by Whom He intends to guide us.
SHAPE informs us:

> Once you have discovered your S.H.A.P.E., God asks you to continue the development process. (Sundquist, op. cit., p. 142.)

> This summary pa`ge will help you capture the essence of what you learned and will help you toward the next step, a ministry mentoring consultation. (Ibid., p. 139.)

The question to be considered is two-fold: Where does the true God "ask" us to begin, let alone "to continue the (SHAPE) development process"? It is not only remarkable but also very significant that the Shape-program stresses this continual development process with a ministry mentoring consultation. Where does that lead? If we remember that every prospective member is to take the Shape-test and must sign a *Membership Covenant,* promising: "I will protect the unity of my church…by following the leaders," and if we also keep in mind that these leaders reflect New Age principles, it will not be so very difficult to get an idea where it ultimately heads to.

We should never allow our faith, teachings, or ministry to rest on the rocky ground of man-made theories and philosophies of worldly wisdom, but solely on the "two edged sword" of God's word.

Only in this way can we escape the current influence of mystical paganism that is gaining so much ground everywhere, including in many of the Christian churches.

Chapter 25

New Age

New Age, Occultism, Witchcraft, Eastern Mysticism, Romanism, Ecumenism, and Freemasonry go hand in hand and have unknowingly invaded many Christian Churches all over the world, and that largely through the modern church-growth movement.

It is from the interlinked occult organisation of Theosophy and Freemasonry that the New Age Movement appeared in the late 1970's. Despite the name, there is nothing new in its teaching, but it is a re-launching of the Occult, witchcraft and Eastern Mysticism under an appealing name. The concept of the New Age comes from Freemasonry. This is best exemplified by the 33rd Degree Masons' publication entitled the *'New Age Magazine'*. Again, the name of this publication has since been changed, so as to conceal the connection between Freemasonry and the New Age. (I. A. Sadler, *Mystery, Babylon the Great*, Cromwell Press, Trowbridge, Wiltshire, UK 2003, p. 247.)

According to the New Age we now live in the Age of Aquarius; the Age of the spirit, in which spiritual experiences are central. In line with this, the *Alpha training manual* also clearly states that we now live in the age of the Spirit. (p. 29.) The Age of Pisces, the period of rationality is past.

A general New Age method to introduce the new mondial spiritual values is to disparage truth and facts. Thus logical reasoning is attacked. Everything is declared in a relative way. Accordingly we often hear statements like: "There is no absolute truth" or "Nobody can say that he has the truth." Why would others, who experience and believe things in a different way, not have the truth? "The idea that all religions, including Christianity each have an element of the truth, originated with Gnosticism, and has since been carried forward by Freemasonry." (Sadler, *op cit.,* p. 244.)

This has led to what is now known as "postmodernism." Postmodernistic truth is related to the community to which one belongs. Foundational truth unrelated to human norms is thus denied. The Protestant concept of priesthood of individual believers who are responsible directly to God is thus denied. Conscience is unacceptable as the basis for determining truth. Relative truth being the only truth available, is seen to relate not to the individual but to the community he is in.

> Truth does not exist. What we find in the world is a host of conflicting viewpoints and interpretations, and linguistically formed worlds, all of which are equally invalid, and thus equally valid... The only valid truth for postmodern adherents is the local narrative of a particular society. Truth is socially conditioned, thus our understanding of truth is conditioned by the community in which we find ourselves. While truth is not universal, postmodernism does not relativise truth to that of each individual, but rather to that of each community. Truth is cultural, and each person participates in that truth. Seeing that there are many cultures, there are many truths... Both our perceptions of truth and the essence of truth are relative. Reality is a human construct determined by the group which guides and even dictates social life, mores, and values. As a result postmodernism has abandoned the Enlightenment quest for a grasp of an objective, unified reality. (Jason Dulle, *The Question of Truth and Apologetics in a Modern-Postmodern World.* Cf., Stanley J. Grenz, *A Primer on Postmodernism, 1996,* p. 14.)

But is there no general standard for that which is truth? Can every community decide on its own what to consider truth? Does this mean that someone who is completely dedicated to God's Word can't testify with certainty that he has the truth? Will not God's promised Spirit guide the sincere believers into **all truth** and give them **assurance**? (Cf., John 16:13)

> It is as certain that we have the truth as that God lives; and Satan, with all his arts and hellish power, cannot change the truth of God into a lie. While the great adversary will try his utmost to make of none effect the word of God, truth must go forth as a lamp that burneth. (*Testimonies for the Church*, vol. 4, p. 595.)

But what is the intended result when everything is relative and there are no fixed and true facts and specifications anymore? "…people can't argue back from a basis of understanding. They will not have an objective framework from which to draw conclusions." Thus the way is open to accept all kinds of new spiritual models of the cultures of this world that are mostly pantheistic and polytheistic.

> What we are seeing is a rise in animistic religions because the Biblical ethic and value system has been not only discarded, but forbidden to be discussed. Is this not similar to what is happening in the churches today? Attempts to hold teachers accountable to God's Word are met with derision, even by those who insist that they believe that God's Word must form the basis for judging all things. We learn quickly that their exhortation to Biblical integrity is merely a ploy to disarm their critics and deceive their listeners. God's Word is valued, yes; but it is placed on the lower order of thinking skills. What is more important is intuitive 'Holy Spirit' power…Many wish to worship God in the Spirit, and this is fine; but they neglect the second requirement: that we worship Him in truth. His Word is truth (John 17:17). The two cannot be separated, for God's work is by His Word. (*Holy Laughter, Rodney Howard-Browne and the Toronto Blessing, Reordered Thinking,* Biblical Discernment Ministries, 3/96. Excerpted and/or adapted from a 4/95 Special Report by the same name from Media Spotlight, Albert James Dager, pp. 25, 26.)

Everybody has to experience the transition or "paradigm shift". Alpha with Nicky Gumbel, Bill Hybels of the Willow Creek Community, and Rick Warren of the Saddleback Church, and other church-growth leaders understand this concept well and they stress that churches also need to go through this transition by becoming less rational and more spiritual for the power and the working of the Spirit must be experienced in a more general way by the churches.

Gumbel writes:

> I have found on Alpha that those from an essentially enlightened background feel at home with the parts of the course which appeal to the mind, but that they often have difficulty in experiencing the Holy Spirit. Others coming from the New Age movement, find that rational and historical explanations leave them cold, but at the weekend away they are on more familiar ground in experiencing the

Holy Spirit. (*Telling Others*, p. 19.)

Should not this alarm us? Those entangled in the spirit of the New Age movement, come with their spiritual experiences and aspirations at Alpha on more **familiar** ground! **This can only mean Alpha and the New Age have common principles, for otherwise there can't be familiar ground.** And this is only possible when the **same** spirit is revealed in both, since there can't be anything familiar between God's Spirit and the spirit of evil. Therefore, it should not surprise us that Alpha's teachings breathe the spirit of the New Age.

McDonald and Peterson, who studied Alpha profoundly, corroborate:

> Indeed, after a thorough analysis of all the Course materials we can confirm that, if one considers the *complete* body of Alpha's teaching on any given issue, *every single one* of its doctrines is *significantly* slanted towards the New Age position. (Elizabeth McDonald and Dusty Peterson, *Alpha The Unofficial Guide,* Cambridge, 2004, p. 159.)

These authors openly warn:

> Clearly, just omitting the 'Holy Spirit weekend' is not a sufficient response by churches tempted to use Alpha. The entire content is steeped in error and thoroughly leavened, thus it *cannot* safely be adapted. (Ibid.)

Thus, far from being set free by Alpha, those coming from the New Age movement are in fact further deceived, while rational explanation does not touch or move them. They are only touched by all kinds of spiritual experiences and wonderful manifestations. They don't worry about knowledge by which they could see and evaluate the whole thing. Their spiritual life appears to be based on carnal or natural instincts and feelings and Alpha does not provide any help but offers familiar ground.

Can one, who has not surrendered himself in faith to God, lead a God-pleasing spiritual life? Can he have genuine, consistent spiritual experiences? If he is not truly converted and has no interest in searching for the truth is he likely to understand the full essence of the gospel? (1 Cor. 2:14.) Explanation doesn't seem to interest him. Indeed, we are informed it even leaves him cold. Could this then relate to true church-growth by which people are sincerely converted? Do people really accept genuine faith merely by spiritual manifestations?

The Bible teaches us: "So then faith cometh by hearing, and hearing by the word of God." (Rom. 10:17).

We don't read that faith is by seeing spiritual manifestations. No! Faith is by hearing the proclamation of the word of God. Jesus gave us a good example to follow. He explained the holy Writings and thus opened truth to the mind:

> Beginning at Moses and all the prophets, he expounded unto them in all the scriptures the things concerning himself...Then opened he their understanding, that they might understand the scriptures. And said unto them, Thus it is written...(Luke 24:27, 45, 46.)

The apostle Paul doesn't place a transforming experience in the working of spiritual manifestations above that of the sound thinking of a rational mind. He clearly admonishes: "...be ye transformed by the renewing of your mind, that ye may prove what is that good, and acceptable, and perfect, will of God." (Rom. 12:2.)

Paul thus identifies a renewed way of thinking and clear perception as the basis for transformation of the life in doing that which is good and perfect.

Nor would the apostle Peter agree with the modern "paradigm shift". On the contrary, he wouldn't allow spiritual manifestations to take a prominent place. He specifically appeals to everybody: "Gird up the loins of your mind, be sober..." (1 Peter 1:13.)

Peter does not expect God's children to stay ready by means of their **feelings**, but to be ready with their **mind**: sober and watchful, so they won't be tossed back and forth by all kinds of teachings, nor being misled and deceived by the miraculous works of spirits of the dark and evil practices of the New Age.

The Alpha course and Nicky Gumbel are a part of the Anglican church which had a worldwide gathering at the "Lambeth Conference" at London in July 1998. Remarkable was the ecumenical spirit revealing itself especially in unity with the Roman Catholic Church and the New Age movement. Some points that were supported by this conference were:

A. The merger with Roman Catholics;
B. The agenda for Interfaith as proposed by the global community;
C. The New Age environmental "Save Mother Earth" propaganda;
D. The New International Economic Order with World Bank;
E. The New Age agenda for the New World Order.

We are seriously warned concerning this conference:

> Bear in mind that what the Lambeth Conference stands for, so does (the) Alpha Course. Nicky Gumble was there at that scandalous conference, under the headship of the Archbishop of Canterbury as an Anglican. So attuned to these New Age NWO plans was Gumble that he actually lectured to the delegates. Can the reader see that Alpha is about Unity in the United Nations occult One World? That INTERFAITH with other religions is behind the curtains, not just the ecumenical movement? (Endtime Ministries, Wendy B. Howard, *The Alpha Course, Friend or Foe?* Appendix 5.)

The keyword for the churches of this present day is **unity** with the goal: believing together and jointly confessing in one huge world-church of love and brotherhood. It seems that in this context every method, every compromise, every kind of cooperation and a farrago of teachings are acceptable. To criticize different deviating teachings or some unbiblical practices, is no longer regarded as useful but is rather seen as loveless. The Biblical way to "reprove, rebuke, exhort with all longsuffering and doctrine," seems to be outmoded and no longer finds approval. (2 Tim. 4:2, 3; Titus 1:9)

Nicky Gumbel, Alpha's author, writes:

> ...we make it a rule on Alpha never to criticize another denomination, another Christian church or a Christian leader. (*Telling Others*, p. 114.)

> Actually we must stop judging one another. (*The Impact of Toronto*, p. 83.)

New Age • 99

> We need to unite…there has been some comment which is not helpful to unity. Let us drop that and get on. It is wonderful that the movement of the Spirit will always bring churches together. He is doing that right across the denominations and within the traditions…we are seeing Roman Catholics coming now…Nobody is suspicious of anybody else…People are no longer 'labeling' themselves or others. I long for the day when we drop all these labels and just regard ourselves as Christians with a commission from Jesus Christ. (*Renewal*, May 1995, p. 16.)

G. A. Pritchard, in an exhaustive study on Willow Creek for his Ph. D. dissertation, touches not only positive things, but also the negative:

> Ironically, while Hybels is evangelizing those in the world toward Christianity, he is also evangelizing Christians toward the world. As the unchurched Harrys in the audience (10 percent) move closer to Christianity, the Christians in the audience (90 percent) are often becoming more psychological and worldly. This tendency to compromise Christian truth is built into this model of the church… The effect of this penetration of the psychological worldview on Willow Creek's teaching is profound. This sort of accomodation 'leads to a disappearing boundary between religious beliefs and other beliefs, thus rendering religion irrelevant because they are indistinguishable from a secular viewpoint.' In the effort to become relevant Willow Creek ironically is in danger of becoming irrelevant. (G. A. Pritchard, *Willow Creek Seeker Services,* Baker Books, 1996, p. 238, 239.)

This is a pretty disturbing portrayal. Most important, however, is the question of to what "Christianity" this model of the church is moving toward? True Christianity? Or a Pagan counterfeit? The answer doesn't seem to be difficult. Moreover, Pritchard's portrayal of the terms of Willow Creek's 12 steps program to help people deal with their problems also suggests a clear answer:

> Even church members could not talk about Christian truth in these meetings at Willow Creek. Although the programs give lip service to a 'Higher Power,' they function as practical atheism, teaching the categories of the contemporary psychological worldview. Yet the lack of theological content did not stop the church from advertising these programs each week during the weekend and

weekday services. That Willow Creek would sponsor and advertise these programs illustrates the church's lack of priority for educating its members in Christian truth. (Ibid., p. 273.)

One would expect the truth of the gospel to be high in the banner of Willow Creek, as it busies itself with all its church-growth programs and activities to establish people in the church. But in practice it appears to be otherwise.

The program for alcoholics, for example, is founded on hypnosis, psychotherapy and faith in a "higher power" to one's own choosing. In search for faith, many different paths can be trodden, so we read. When the road that is offered, isn't pleasing, then the person can discover something else that will satisfy him. It is also possible, if someone would wish that, to trust and have faith in the program itself and make that as his "higher power." (*Twelve Steps and Twelve Traditions*, p. 26, 27.)

It doesn't seem to matter much if people choose to follow false gods. As long as it has effect and works well, it is not regarded as a problem. No wonder Dave Hunt reproaches Hybels and Willow Creek, and other churches because they apply this "deadly delusion," thus supporting it rather than warning against it. (*Occult Invasion*, Harvest House Publ., Eugene, Oregon, 1998, p. 294.)

In this time of the end a clear warning message must be given. Falsehood will be so mingled with truth that only by the Word of the Lord and the guidance of the Holy Spirit truth can be distinguished from error. The wide spread fine-tuned spiritual influence of the New Age movement is very dramatic and highly alarming.

> Right now—more than any period in the Christian church—the body of Christ is experiencing an overkill of spiritual deception that is so fine-tuned it is becoming difficult to detect. Christians are suffering from toxic levels of compromise, and causing other Christians to stumble. Silver-tongued wolves have sheepishly grinned and smiled their way into the Christian Church by paying lip-service to Jesus Christ, while being an intrinsic part of the New Age Movement at the same time. (*Ken Blanchard Still Endorsing the New Age,* Christian Research Service, Update on Ken Blanchard #3, February 11, 2006. p. 1.)

G. Kumar, a prominent New Age leader,

...defines the New Age Movement as a 'Paradigm Shift to Divine Consciousness' and '...a revival of spiritual and divine values and can be called as a Divine Regeneration Movement. New Age Philosophy has conquered the West intellectually and Western culture is currently experiencing a phenomenal shift-sociological, spiritual & ideological. It's a secular, multi-cultural, multi-religious synthesis, of the Oriental mystical philosophies, mainly Hinduism, Buddhism, Taoism & Western Occultism, emphasising Holism, the doctrine that Reality is organically One. (Ibid., p. 2.)

Just to get an idea of the alarming influence, we are informed that "there are 6 million New Age sites on the Web" while the movement,

...consists of a massive and well organised network...of thousands of groups, trusts, foundations, clubs, lodges, and spiritual groups whose goal and purpose is to prepare the world to enter the coming Aquarian Age...New Age practices have almost conquered the world. Athletes are using guided imagery. Graduate schools of business are invoking TM, Yoga, and Tarot cards in teaching courses on creativity in business... (Ibid.)

Kumar, being deeply entrenched in the New Age, explains how the movement has infiltrated the secular and Christian world:

Significant influence has been gained by NAM (New Age Movement) affecting almost every area of Occidental culture—Sociology, Psychology, Medicine, the Government, Ecology, Science, Arts, Education, the Business Community, the media, entertainment, sports, **and even the Church**. Organised spiritual forms such as Christian Science, Unity and even forms of Witchcraft (from the German ' Wicca' meaning the Wise; Witchcraft means the Craft of the Wise) are all its expressions. Various **Human Potential Seminars**, Transcendental Meditation, Zen Meditation, and some Alternative Holistic Medicine practices are also its manifold manifestations. (Ibid., p. 3, Emphasis present.)

Six main characteristics of New Age thinking are presented by Kumar that deserve serious attention of each sincere Christian: "(1) All is Unity; (2) All is Divine; (3) Humanity is divine; (4) A change in Consciousness; (5) All religions are One; and (6) Cosmic Evolutionary optimism." (Ibid.)

It must be clear then that the New Age echoes the old serpent's lie in declaring mankind divine. And we all need a 'paradigm shift'—a change in consciousness—a difference of attitude and beliefs. Sadly, these New Age characteristics infiltrated the church growth movement and have entered many churches around the world.

Chapter 26

Traditional and Modern Magic

A careful look at Rick Warren's book *The Purpose Driven Life* reveals the introduction of New Age concepts. The very first Bible text mentioned in Chapter 1 deviates clearly and fundamentally from the true word of the Gospel. We read: "For everything, absolutely everything, above and below, visible and invisible,...everything got started in him and finds its purpose in him." (Col. 1:16 (*Msg*)).

This text from the paraphrased *Message Bible* by Eugene Peterson, seriously distorts what the Bible really says. The word "purpose" for instance, is not in the original text and neither are the words "above" and "below" for the words are "heaven" and "earth." Even in the Lord's Prayer: "Thy will be done in earth, as it is in heaven," are the words heaven and earth changed into: "as above, so below."

But isn't heaven above and earth below? What difference does it really make? In answer we need to consider two other questions: What is the purpose of this change? Is it merely accidental?

Janet Moser presents a list of more than 30 examples and points of direct or indirect links of this Bible with different mystical and occult people and organizations and concludes: "Through the use of paraphrase, *'The Message'* was 'crafted' to present the doctrines of mysticism to the Christian church in order to seduce believers into the occult and the New Age Movement." (*The Mystical Bible, The Message of Mysticism*, p. 1.)

Moser presents a number of significant factors of the hidden agenda:

A. Christianity must embrace mysticism;
B. Doctrines about the Bible rejected;
C. Bible to be interpreted and taught allegorically, not literally;
D. Christian doctrine to be changed;
E. New Bibles will contain new Gospel and new message;
F. Mysticism to be taught in Christian and Jewish seminaries;
G. Mysticism to be made accessible to average person;
H. Those teaching mysticism to the Church will deny it;
I. New Age mysticism to be promoted by the Church and Masonry;
J. Mysticism will become the universal religion through the ecumenical movement;
K. World Bible to be based on mysticism.

Is it accidental or is it Purpose Driven that Rick Warren quotes *The Message* 83 times in his book: *The Purpose Driven Life?* This paraphrased bible is clearly in harmony with New Age Mysticism. It is absolutely no accident that the clear words heaven and earth even in Our Lord's Prayer and in Col. 1:16 are changed into the significant, pregnant, magical words: "above and below."

We have only to check the internet and type the words "as above, so below" in the "google" search machine, and the very first result will give us sufficient information:

'As above, so below'

> "As above, so below"…"That which is above is the same as that which is below" (www.themystica.com/mystica/articles/a/below_above.html)
>
> This phrase comes from the beginning of The Emerald Tablet and embraces the entire system of traditional and modern magic which was inscribed upon the tablet in cryptic wording by Hermes Trismegistus. The significance of this phrase is that it is believed to hold the key to all mysteries. All systems of magic are claimed to function by this formula. "That which is above is the same as that which is below"…Macrocosmos is the same as microcosmos. The universe is the same as God, God is the same as man, man is the same as the cell, the cell is the same as the atom, the atom is the same as…and so on, ad infinitum.
>
> This message theorizes that man is the counterpart of God on earth; as God is man's counterpart in heaven. Therefore, it is a state-

ment of an ancient belief that man's actions on earth parallel the actions of God in heaven. This pivots on the belief that "all things have their birth from this One Thing by adaptation."

To the magician the magical act, that of causing a transformation in a thing or things without any physical contact, is accomplished by an imaginative act accompanied by the will that the wanted change will occur. The magical act and imaginative act becomes one and the same. The magician knows with certainty that for the change to occur he must will it to happen and firmly believe it will happen. Here it may be noted that magic and religion are akin: both require belief that a miracle will occur.

To bring about such a change the magician uses the conception of "dynamic interconnectedness to describe the physical world as the sort of thing that imagination and desire can effect. The magician's world is an independent whole, a web of which no strand is autonomous. Mind and body, galaxy and atom, sensation and stimulus, are intimately bound. Witchcraft strongly imbues the view that all things are independent and interrelated." These concepts pivot on the belief that all things come from the One Thing, or First Cause, and "Its power is integrating, if it be turned into earth."

The purpose of all rituals in ceremonial magic is to unite the microcosm with the macrocosm to join God, or gods when invoked, with the human consciousness. When such a supreme union is achieved the subject and object becomes one. This is because the magician feels that he is consciously in touch with all elements of the universe, therefore, he can control them. It may be said, the magician feels connected with the universe. This feeling intensifies the more the magician successfully practices his skills. Whenever he experiences a failure he knows that the ritual was not performed correctly. **[Note: This underlies the practice of modern meditation.]**

When feeling unison with the universe the magician knows he has reached his Higher or True Self because he has attained mastery of himself and the universe. Thus he feels his "skillful work ascends from earth to heaven and descends to earth again, and receives the power of the superiors and of the inferiors." Therefore, he "hast the glory of the whole world therefore let all obscurity flee from thee." Now the miracles are possible.

Some magicians, including Aleister Crowley, claimed that when the magician reaches this ultimate peak of altered consciousness the miracles are no longer important, the extreme goal becomes the direct union with God. *A.G.H. (Internet article with Note added.)*

This specific phrase "as above so below" comes from "The Emerald Tablet" and, as we have read: **"embraces the entire system of traditional and modern magic."**

It is a serious matter that this telling phrase is introduced into God's holy word and even used in Our Lord's Prayer. It is a bad sign that Rick Warren so often quotes this New Age bible. It is not surprising, however, for we are informed that Rick Warren works together with Ken Blanchard who favours New Age teachings, Mantra meditation, Yoga, and Buddhism.

> Blanchard makes no apology when he says much can be gained from Buddhism. He and his wife both encourage the practice of yoga and mantra meditation.
>
> Even more disturbing is his seat on the Board of Advisors of a New Age organization called Hoffman's Institute. (*Lighthouse Trails Research Project*, April 19, 2005. *'Rick Warren Teams Up With New-Age Guru Ken Blanchard!* This is a Special Report.')

However, Rick Warren of Saddleback is not alone; he and Bill Hybels of Willow Creek work together in his association with Blanchard as close team players:

> Ken Blanchard, Rick Warren and Bill Hybels (Willow Creek) have become team players at the Lead Like Jesus conferences and the Leadership Summit conferences which take place across North America. The three also have an audio set they co-authored together. Incidentally, Rick Warren sits on the Board of Blanchard's Lead Like Jesus organization along with Ken Blanchard, Mark Victor Hansen (Chicken Soup for the Soul), John Maxwell, Bill Hybels, and Laurie Beth Jones. (Ibid.)

It is interesting to note that the spiritual story books *Chicken Soup for the Soul* by Jack Canfield and Mark Victor Hansen come from a New Age background, since both authors reveal and promote their Occultic New Age ideas.

> It is apparent the underlying theme of Canfield and Hansen's comments are the avocation of moving people towards New Age mysticism. This should be alarming to Christians in light of the

popularity of these authors. (Ray Yungen, *A Time of Departing*, Silverton, Oregon, 2002, p. 88.)

Chapter 27

New Age Pantheism

Warren writes in his book *The Purpose Driven Life* on page 88: "The Bible says, 'He rules everything and is everywhere and is in everything.'"

The Message Bible, Rick Warren uses, may say this. But it is not only unbiblical; it is a purely pantheistic thought promoted today by the New Age—a revival of the old philosophical system of divination of nature; a oneness of God with everything and everybody. This thought is clearly presented in Lesson 29 of the New Age: *A Course in Miracles* with the title: "God is in everything I see," Significantly the word "purpose" particularly stressed by Warren, is prevalent throughout this Lesson's teaching. (Warren Smith, *Deceived on Purpose, The New Age Implications of the Purpose-Driven Chrurch,* Second Edition, 2005, p. 81.)

Since we now live in the Aquarian Age, signifying that the human race is entering a "Golden Age," certain transitions must take place.

> ...during these transitions certain cosmic influences begin to flow into the mass consciousness of mankind and cause changes to occur...This...'planetary transformation'...will bring 'universal oneness' to all mankind. The view is that as more and more members of the human race 'attune' themselves to 'Aquarian energies,' the dynamics of the 'old age' will begin to fade out.
>
> Just what 'energies' are we supposed to be attuning ourselves to? New Age thought teaches that everything that exists, seen or unseen, is made up of energy—tiny particles of vibrating energy, atoms, molecules, protons, etc. All is energy. That energy, they believe, is God, and therefore, **all is God**. They believe that since we are all part of this 'God-energy,' then **we, too are God**. God is not

seen as a Being that dwells in heaven, but as the universe itself... The Age of Aquarius is when we are all supposed to come to the **understanding that man is God.** The goal in the New Age of Aquarius will be **how to bring this idea into meaningful reality.** (Ray Yungen, *For Many Shall Come In My Name, How mainstream America is accepting the 'Ancient Wisdom' teaching and what this foreshadows.* Solid Rock, Woodburn, Oregon, Second Printing, Revised Ed., 1991, pp. 5, 6.)

The warnings of the word of God regarding the perils surrounding the Christian church belong to us today. As in the days of the apostles, men tried by tradition and philosophy to destroy faith in the Scriptures, so today, by the pleasing sentiments of higher criticism, evolution, spiritualism, theosophy, and pantheism, the enemy of righteousness is seeking to lead souls into forbidden paths. To many the Bible is as a lamp without oil, because they have turned their minds into channels of speculative belief that brings misunderstanding and confusion. (E. G. White, *The Acts of the Apostles*, p. 474.)

On the very first page of the introduction to Warren's book *The Purpose Driven Life*, we find another curious New Age phenomenon. Consider these words: "This book is dedicated to you. Before you were born, God planned **this moment** in your life. It is no accident that you are holding this book."

These pregnant words covertly glorify the book that is held to be so exceptional that before you were even born and when, understandably, the book did not yet exist, God foreordained not only its publication, which thus can be no accident, but also the very moment you would hold it in your hands.

It is true that God's care and leading of true believers is great. Yet we cannot accept these pregnant words without close examination, for there is more going on in the conflict between good and evil than God's providential working. For our great adversary, who goes about as a roaring lion, also reveals himself as an angel of light. Wouldn't it be possible for him to play a decisive role in claiming to divine providence for his delusions? Does he not delight when we hold a misleading book in our hands, hoping we will receive it as from God?

Indeed, note that Warren's words seem to be an echo from Neale

Donald Walsch, a prominent leader of the New Age. In his book *Conversations with God,* book 2, 1997, he assures:

> This book has arrived in your life at the right and perfect time... Everything happens in perfect order, and the arrival of this book in your life is no exception.

These words breathe clearly the same thought as expressed by Warren. There is no question of accident—all things are disposed—the book comes exactly on the right moment—everything happens according to a plan—and so everything is purpose driven; as well as our lives.

To many, Warren's books may sound good, but we must remember that the Bible says: "There is a way that seemeth right unto a man, but the end thereof are the ways of death." (Proverbs 16:25.) **Truth and error may be presented very close and almost indistinguishable together.**

> As we near the end of time, falsehood will be so mingled with truth, that only those who have the guidance of the Holy Spirit will be able to distinguish truth from error...Those who are guided by the Word of the Lord will discern with certainty between falsehood and truth, between sin and righteousness. (MS 43, 1907. *EGW Comments* on Colossians 2:8.)

Chapter 28

Occultism

It is quite remarkable how great the similarities are between the modern church-growth movement and the occult ideas as they are proclaimed by the New Age movement. We have God's reliable Word in which the great apostasy of the last days clearly is revealed. The question is asked: "when the Son of man cometh, shall He find faith on the earth?" (Luke 18:8).

Will the church-growth movement so greatly applauded in these last days lead the great multitudes to the true faith or will they be led on a wrong track?

"...and all the world wondered after the beast...and the dragon gave him his power, and his seat, and great authority...And they worshipped the dragon...that old serpent, called the devil and satan, which deceiveth the whole world." And Babylon "is become the habitation of devils and the hold of every foul spirit." (Rev. 13:1-3; 12:9; 18:2.)

In the great controversy between good and evil, we have, on the one hand, the revelations God has given us, while on the other hand, there are the occult messages from the army camp of the devil. Alice Bailey, a New Age high priest and one of the main mediums has, through higher telepathy, revealed the occultic New Age ideas. She revealed as the New World Religion the revival of the old Babylonian and pagan forms of worship, which are known and accepted in our days as "Christian". She also gives some interesting information about the near coming of the cosmic Christ:

> His coming is largely dependent...upon the establishing of right human relations. This the church has hindered down the centuries, and has not helped because of its fanatical zeal to make 'Chris-

tians' of all peoples and not followers of the Christ. It has emphasised theological doctrine, and not love and loving understanding as Christ exemplified it. The Church has preached the fiery Saul of Tarsus and not the gentle Carpenter of Galilee. (*The Reappearance of the Christ*, Lucis Press, p. 12.)

It isn't difficult to recognize, that the points, mentioned here, have taken shape in Alpha, Willow Creek, Saddleback and other modern church-growth movements worldwide.

Among all these "purpose driven" activities, the central theme is that a good human interdenominational relation is built on unity, love and brotherhood. Criticism of other people's beliefs or way of living is loveless and considered inappropriate.

Should we then close our ears and eyes to issues of faith and way of living? Is that the true love shown us in the Bible? How does love reveal itself, according to the Scriptures? We read:

And this I pray, that your love may abound yet more and more in knowledge and in all judgement; that ye may approve things that are excellent; that ye may be sincere and without offence till the day of Christ. (Phil. 1:9, 10.)

Love reveals itself in knowledge, judgement and approval of things that are excellent. May we serve others with this when we see them erring? Is it loveless if we warn and discipline someone in an appropriate way?

Paul declares:

Whereas the aim of the Christian discipline is the love that springs from a pure heart, from a good conscience, and from a sincere faith. Certain individuals have failed here by turning to empty argument; doctors of the Law is what they want to be, but they have no idea either of the meaning of the words they use or of the themes on which they harp. (1 Tim. 1:5–7, Moffatt translation.)

Proper warning and discipline of the unfaithful, springs from a pure and loving heart. Would it not be loveless not to warn those who err and live in violation of God's will and are thus heading for destruction? Are we not for their sakes responsible to raise our voices against "whatever else is contrary to sound doctrine as laid down by that glorious gospel of the blessed God..." (vs. 10, 11.)

Those who faithfully do this, should be highly esteemed:

> We beseech you, brethren, to know them which labour among you, and are over you in the Lord, and admonish you; and to esteem them very highly in love for their work's sake. And be at peace among yourselves. Now we exhort you, brethren, warn them that are unruly, comfort the feebleminded, support the weak, be patient toward all men. (1 Thess. 5:12–14.)

To the contrary, Gumbel, Alpha's great teacher has made it a rule not to make any comment on others, no matter what they believe or teach. Such practices should be stopped.

Gumbel's issue is that all church walls should be broken down. Theological doctrine should not be stressed and there should be no zeal to win souls from other churches.

But the Bible explains that those need discipline who are vain babblers, having no idea either of the meaning of the words they use or of the themes on which they harp.

New Age high priestess, Bailey, also describes other matters that clearly find response in today's modern churches. We read for example:

> The church must show a wide tolerance, and teach no revolutionary doctrines or cling to any reactionary ideas... Eventually, there will appear the Church Universal, and its definite outlines will appear towards the close of this (20th) Century. (*The Externalisation of the Hierarchy*, p. 510.)

Note further a few more exerpts from Bailey:

> But—there has been a useful and wholesome swing away from Churchianity and from orthodox religion during the past century, and this will present a unique opportunity for the restoration of true religion and the presentation of a simple return to the ways of spiritual living. (*The Reappearance of the Christ*, p. 17.)

> ...the spiritualists have laid the emphasis upon the aliveness of those who have passed over into the hidden world of being, and their Guides have also borne testimony to the existence of an inner, spiritual world. (Ibid., p. 19, 20.)

> We are suffering theologically from the ignorance of the past; it is a peculiar thing that an ancient commentator is supposed to carry greater weight than the modern, more educated and intelligent man. (Ibid., p. 24.)

> The long divorce between religion and politics must be ended and this can now come about... (Ibid., p. 18.)

It is striking that sincere Christians in various churches who adhere to the orthodox confession of faith are increasingly subject to ridicule in this time of the end. And is it not revealing that while tolerance in the churches is in general a popular word, it reflects an "intolerant tolerance" towards orthodoxy?

> Rick Warren's approach to church growth stems from his primary philosophy: **man-centered pragmatism.** From that faulty foundation arises a ridicule of the old fashioned, and a disdain for the fundamentalist / separatist. (*The Church Growth Movement...* Compiled by Japie Grobler, Review by Rick Meisel, Kies-Ciec, Edleen, South Africa, p. 46.)

It is also conspicuous that old commentators and pioneers who served God faithfully and built up the church in full dedication, seem to be robbed of their splendour. Their insights are, in the light of the "wisdom" of this age, often declared to be outmoded and insignificant. But how deceiving, for not this modern century, nor scholarship or intelligence, no, "the fear of the Lord is the beginning of wisdom." (Prov. 1:7; 9:10.)

On the one hand it is noteworthy that in the modern church-growth movement certain insights and doctrines are unacceptable, while, on the other hand, remarkably enough, every religious thought is easily accepted without any difficulty.

> The problem with the Willow Creek method, however, is that they have opened their doors wide open to ALL religious thought (including secular thought), and embraced them under the guise of Christian love and acceptance, even when it is diametrically opposed to the fundamentals of Christianity. (Chris Carmicheal, *The Willow Creek Dilemma*, Aug. 2001, p. 12, Conclusion, Paragraph 2.)

The criterion, evidently, is not so much whether it is truth, but rather if it is more appealing and satisfying in order to reach as many people as possible. Unity of all religions in one world-church is the goal pursued. The emphasis is on the spiritual; the hidden spiritual world. With occultist New Agers, the singular goal is that this age of the spirit should take more and more shape in the churches and in politics.

For political governments are also more and more involved with religion as they play a part behind the scenes. Satan carefully devised a broad master plan, in which,

> ...education, governments, churches, theology, philosophy, psychology, science and culture take a part. Startling developments within this plan are emerging from liberal Roman Catholicism amalgamated with the Eastern religions. (*Freedom's Ring*, Sept. 1991, vol. 2, no 8, p. 2.)

Catholicism, Eastern religions and politics will play their part and it is significant that the church growth movement particularly co-operates with Catholicism and introduces Eastern meditative practices and incorporates politics. She seeks to unite religions and to realize co-operation between church and state and the economical world.

Rick Warren testifies:

> I am looking to build bridges with the Orthodox Church — looking to build bridges with the Catholic Church—with the Anglican Church. (*Anglican Conference*, Nov., 2005.)

Note his close co-operation with the Catholic church:

> Actually, we're working on the Catholic workbook for the "Purpose Driven Life" that has been written by some priests in America. I asked Cardinal Rosales if somebody could review it and tell us what needed to be changed before it went to print and he could give the blessing that it was okay, that it was for all Catholic congregations, cathedrals, churches, chapels. (*Philippine Daily Inquirer*, July 30, 2006. p. C1.)

As for his involvement with business and government leaders Warren explains:

I have trained around 400,000 pastors in 162 countries. But now, my staff and I are not just training church leaders but business and government leaders and helping them, too…

A three-legged stool will have stability. So I'm going from country to country teaching business its role, teaching church its role, and teaching government leaders their role—you've got to work together. (Ibid.)

Consider in this framework Ellen White's warning and note the result that will follow when, united with Rome, church and government work together:

> The mingling of church craft and state craft is represented by the iron and the clay. [Dan. 2:41–45] This union is weakening all the power of the churches. This investing the church with the power of the state will bring evil results. Men have almost passed the point of God's forbearance. They have invested their strength in politics, and have united with the papacy. (*Manuscript Releases*. Vol. I, Silver Spring, MD, 1981, p. 51.)

> The union of the church with the state, be the degree never so slight, while it may appear to bring the world nearer to the church, does in reality but bring the church nearer to the world. (*The Great Controversy*, p. 297.)

> Protestant churches that have followed in the steps of Rome by forming alliance with worldly powers have manifested a similar desire to restrict liberty of conscience… When the leading churches of the United States, uniting upon such points of doctrine as are held by them in common, shall influence the state to enforce their decrees and to sustain their institutions, then Protestant America will have formed an image of the Roman hierarchy, and the infliction of civil penalties upon dissenters will inevitably result. (Ibid., pp. 443, 445.)

The last pieces of End-time Bible prophecy fall into place. Churches go together. Eastern meditative practices evoke occultism and spiritualism worldwide. Co-operation with state-governments will lead to restrict conscience and condemn dissenters. The pursued universal Purpose Driven PEACE plan, supposed to usher in the much desired millennium, will only end up in apostasy.

...Satan determines to unite them in one body and thus strengthen his cause by sweeping all into the ranks of spiritualism...Papists, Protestants, and worldlings will alike accept the form of godliness without the power, and they will see in this union a grand movement for the conversion of the world and the ushering in of the long-expected millennium. (Ibid., pp. 588, 589.)

Chapter 29

Freemasonry

Not only is clear harmony seen among Occultism, the New Age and Freemasonry, but striking similarities between these and the present church-growth movement reveals their great influence on the Christian churches.

> Careful examination of Masonic writings show that the leading teachers and Masonic authorities, such as Pike, secretly teach that the god of Freemasonry is Lucifer. It is from Freemasonry that the current New Age movement and Occult societies have developed. These look to the mysterious 'Force' of the supernatural. Lest readers doubt the relevance to Christians…we will state once again that many professedly Christian churches are rife with Freemasonry. (I. A. Sadler, *Mystery, Babylon the Great*, Cromwell Press, Trowbridge, Wiltshire, England, Reprint 2003, p. 184.)

From God's Word we know that Satan reveals himself as an angel of light and that he goes around as a roaring lion. He will try everything to succeed and leave no instrument unused to achieve his goal. New Age high priestess Bailey points to the authority of the church to heal and to the brotherhood of the Freemasonry to bring about the one Universal Church. She says:

> Definite work must also be done in healing, in exorcising, in curing mental and astral diseases, and it must be demonstrated to the world that the ancient power to heal still lies in the hands of those who consistently follow the Christ…and the power of the church to heal must be demonstrated. The three main channels through which the preparation for the new age is going on might be regarded as the Church, the Masonic Fraternity and the educational field.
> The Masonic Movement…is the custodian of the law; it is the

home of the Mysteries and the seat of initiation. It holds in its symbolism the ritual of Deity, and the way of salvation is pictorially preserved in its work. The methods of Deity are demonstrated in its Temples, and under the All-seeing Eye the work can go forward. It is a far more occult organization than can be realized, and is intended to be the training school for the coming advanced occultists. In its ceremonials, lies hidden the wielding of the forces connected with the growth and life of the kingdoms of nature and the unfoldment of the divine aspects in man. In the comprehension of its symbolism will come the power to cooperate with the divine plan. It meets the need of those who work on the first Ray of Will or Power...There is no dissociation between the One Universal Church, the sacred inner Lodge of all true Masons, and the innermost circles of the esoteric societies. (*The Externalisation of the Hierarchy*, pp. 511, 513, 516.)

The power of the church to heal, as proclaimed by New Agers, is clearly emphasized and applied by the modern church-growth movement. Willow Creek, Saddleback and the Alpha course devote more time to the gifts of the Spirit than to a sincere conversion to Christ.

Alpha presents the gospel at times, but its "conversion" is more to a Christian lifestyle than to Christ the way, the truth, and the life; and its major aim is impartation of "supernatural power," especially healing and speaking in tongues. Participants look forward above all to the big weekend when they will receive Holy Spirit empowerment. I remember the 'testimony' of a man devoted to Eastern Mysticism who 'got the Holy Spirit' that weekend—but clearly remained unsaved. (*The Berean Call*, May 2004.)

The influence of Freemasonry on the churches is much greater than we realize. Many church-growth leaders occupy a high position within this organization. It is said that from the Southern Baptist Convention alone, more than one million are members of Freemasonry. Of the preachers 15% and of the deacons 18%. And the warning is given:

Masons are not a harmless fraternity but indeed a dangerous religion. Its own books say it is a religion. It teaches that Jesus is not God and that a person must work his way to heaven. (*International Social Pulse*, August 2002.)

Of themselves they declare:

> Masonry has nothing whatever to do with the Bible; it is not founded upon the Bible. If it was, it would not be Masonry, it would be something else. (George Wingate Chase, *The Digest of Masonic Law*, Pollard & Leighton, Boston, Mass., 1874, pp. 207, 208.)

R. Morris explains how it is possible that everyone, irrespective of any religion, works harmoniously together in the system of Masonry:

> So broad is the religion of Masonry, and so carefully are all sectarian tenets excluded from the system, that the Christian, the Jew, and the Mohammedan, in all their numberless sects and divisions, may, and do harmoniously combine in its moral and intellectual work with the Buddhist, the Parsee, the Confucian, and the worshiper of Deity under every form. (Rob Morris, *Webb's Monitor of Freemasonry*, p. 280.)

Edmond Ronayne declares:

> The religion of Masonry is a system of absolute despotism, and like that of Rome, demands a blind unquestioning obedience to all its laws, rules, and edicts, whether 'right or wrong'…The religion of Masonry is both unscriptural and antiscriptural, and like Romanism, wholly based on corrupt traditions. (*The Master's Carpet, Masonry & Baal-worship Identical*, Ch. T. Powner Co., 1879, reprint, 2002, Crown Rights Book Comp., p. 69, 77.)

Comparing this system with the Bible, Ronayne testifies:

> But Freemasonry 'carefully excludes' the Lord Jesus Christ from the Lodge and chapter, repudiates his mediatorship, rejects his atonement, denies and disowns his gospel, frowns upon his religion and his church, ignores the Holy Spirit, and sets up for itself a spiritual empire, a religious theocracy, at the head of which it places the G.A.O.T.U.—the god of nature—and from which the one only living and true God is expelled by resolution; and by virtue of the silly ceremonies of this religious system, it professes to renew man's nature and secure for him in the hereafter a happy immortality in 'the Grand Lodge above.' (Ibid., p. 87.)

The great benefit to be derived from obedient affiliation with the system of Freemasonry in lodge worship is freedom from sin and being saved. This in fact is similar to the Roman Catholic doctrine of salvation by works. Sources of this system clearly state that a Mason, "by living in strict obedience to the obligations and precepts of the fraternity is free from sin." (Ibid., p. 98, 102, 105. Albert Gallatin Mackey, *A Lexicon of Freemasonry,* NewYork, 1845; Philadelphia, 1855, See under "Acacian".)

Note the agreement between the Romish and Masonic systems,

> According to the Romish system, a man is purified and made holy by the ceremonies of the chapel; according to the Masonic system, he is made pure and holy and spiritually intelligent by the ceremonials of the lodge and by the pagan jugglery of the Hiram Abiff [represents the Sun-god] tragedy. (Ronayne, *The Master's Carpet,* p. 95.)

A Mason is always bound to submit without question to the will or decree of the Master or his superior in the lodge, regardless if it be "right or wrong":

> We may not call in question the propriety of this organization if we would be Masons we must yield private judgment. (Arthur T. C. Pierson, *Traditions of Freemasonry & Its Coincidences With the Ancient Mysteries,* 1865, p. 30.)

Freemasonry clearly is a counterfeit system originating in the Ancient Mysteries of pagan worship:

> In every symbol, ceremony and emblem of Freemasonry, we meet nothing but the *sun-god*—the 'Ancient initiations'—the 'Ancient Mysteries'—the old secret worship of Baal. (Edmond Ronayne, *The Master's Carpet,* p. 306.)

In fact, Freemasonry, by all it accredited authorities, claims to be a revival of the ancient religious philosophy of Egypt, Phoenicia, and other pagan nations, who practiced a secret worship in honor of the sun-god… (Ibid., backcover.)

Pierson openly declares:

> The writings of the ancient sages afford many coincidences in ceremonies, customs, usages, symbols, and allegories, between the ancient mystic, or religious associations, (the Mysteries,) and that which is now termed Freemasonry. (Pierson, *Traditions of Freemasonry,* p. 8.)

After citing several sources, Dr. Burns concludes,

> So, by Masonic testimony, Masonry is founded on the principles of magic and occultism! It should be plain, then, that Masonry is an occult religion and is not compatible at all with Biblical Christianity! (Dr. C. Burns, *Hidden Secrets of Masonry*, Sharing, Mt. Carmel, PA., 1990, p. 33.)

Dr. I. A. Sadler's earlier quoted book was written to warn the Protestant churches against the dangers of the false religion that originated at Babylon. It seeks to trace this through the Bible and secular history, so as to expose the true origin and nature of the Church of Rome and the European Union, with the Pope shown to be Antichrist. Connections between Rome and the occult movements such as Freemasonry, New Age, and the New World Order are clearly shown.

During the last Centuries Jesuits took over commanding positions within Masonry and via the Illuminati added extra tiers above it, so that Freemasonry was made a strong tool and instrument in the hands of Rome. Note the following quote:

> ...the links between revolutionary Freemasonry and the Jesuits re-appear with surprising and alarming regularity as we go into the 20th century...At the same time as the Church of Rome was gaining ground in the 19th Century, there occurred the so-called 'Occult Explosion.' This was a great proliferation of new occult societies and groups, including those who openly declared that they worshiped Lucifer and practiced witchcraft. The book on Freemasonry edited by Dekker provides very detailed references and extensive evidence to show that all these occult groups were derived from and linked to the highest levels of Freemasonry. As well as their common connection with Freemasonry, they all represented a return to the pagan religion of the Mysteries." (I. A. Sadler, *Mystery, Babylon the Great*, Cromwell Press, Trowbridge, Wiltshire, Reprint 2003, pp. 201, 210, 211. Privately published. The author was awarded an Honorary Doctorate of Literature in October 2000 by the European Theological Seminary in recognition of this book.)

Freemasonry and Catholicism contain old Babylonian characteristics and although Rome has condemned Freemasonry in the past, there is a strong bond, especially also with the Roman Catholic organization Opus Dei. Saussy concludes that Rome's condemnation was a deliberate ploy to hide its use of Freemasonry in attacking the Protestant cause. (F. Tupper Saussy, *Rulers of Evil*, Ospray, 1999, p. 120.) Many Catholic leaders seem to be members. Innumerable prelates, cardinals, archbishops and the leaders of the various Vatican institutions appear to play a prominent part in Freemasonry. The July 1976 "*Bulletin de L'Occident Chrétien*" Nr. 12/12, identified more than hundred Catholic leaders as Masons. (*Alpha, the Unofficial Guide*, p. 183.)

New Age high priestess, Alice Bailey, writes: "There is no dissociation between the One Universal Church, the sacred inner Lodge of all true Masons, and the innermost circles of the esoteric societies." (*The Externalisation of the Hierarchy*, p. 513.)

> "There are many activities on the astral plane. Countless angels, as well as the Master angels of higher order are very busy, angels of devotion...work with the astral bodies of all those who are ready to strengthen and redirect their spiritual aspiration and desire. They are the angels who guard the sanctuaries of all the churches, cathedrals, temples, and mosques of the world. They are now increasing the momentum of their vibration for the raising of the consciousness of the attendant congregations. The Master K. H. works also with the prelates of the great Catholic Churches—Greek, Roman, and Anglican—with the leaders of the Protestant communions, with the foremost workers in the field of education, and also through, and with, the dominant demagogues and organisers of the people." (Ibid., p. 505, 506.)

No wonder then that the Bible describes Babylon—the endtime world church of the New Age, in particular, which is supported by occult and political powers—as a "habitation of devils and the hold of every foul spirit." (Rev. 18:2.)

Ellen White writes: "An innumerable host of evil angels are spreading over the whole land and crowding the churches." (*Early Writings*, p. 274.)

Should it surprise us then to see that the churches and the church-growth movement manifest resemblances with the occultic New Age movement in which Catholicism is leading?

Both Jesuit and Dominican priests occupy important positions within the New Age. The Jesuit Teilhard de Chardin was a leading follower who had great influence. And the Dominican priest, Matthew Fox, holds a prominent place within the New Age, creating and favouring mystic spirituality and seeking to accelerate the coming of the cosmic Christ, who is not human, nor divine, but, according to a third nature, will be cosmic. *(The Coming of the Cosmic Christ,* Harper & Row, 1988, p. 83.)

Fox describes that the world, including the churches, must be prepared for the coming cosmic Christ. He declares that acceptance of the cosmic Christ means a radical change: a "paradigm shift," the transition to a living, spiritual cosmology including a transition from rationalism to mysticism; from religion to spirituality; from obedience, as a main moral virtue, to creativity as most important moral quality; from personal salvation to joint healing; from a personal Saviour to a cosmic Christ; from theïsm to pantheïsm. (Ibid., pp. 134, 135.)

Not the Muslim religion but Roman Catholicism takes the lead in this drastic, globalising, spiritual-religious revolution. Catholicism represents the church and usurps the right to represent the state as well. It plays—also because of the influential role of Mary—as no other power, a part in the affairs of the world.

"The pope is well placed to emerge as spiritual leader of the New Age movement..." (M. de Semlyen, *All Roads lead to Rome*, p. 100.)

[Remember the Popes deny the Father and the Son by taking their place on earth as "Holy Father" and as "Vicar of Christ"—a characteristic of the Antichrist. 1 John 2:22.]

> Like the Vatican, the New Age has close links with powerful organizations such as the United Nations, UNESCO, the World Council of Churches, the Club of Rome, the Trilateral commission, the Bilderberg Group and the Freemasons. Other organizations and movements with a political agenda, such as the conservationist and the many and various peace and disarmament groups, also act as a veil behind which one world-government and one-world religion are taking shape...Mary, the Mother and Virgin Queen, has near universal appeal. She is already playing a major role in helping to bring together a one-world religion, and is certainly attracting New Age devotees too. (Ibid., pp. 100, 101.)

It is not surprising that the church-growth movement is tightly connected with Catholicism. The Vatican is very positive and enthusiastic about Alpha and has its own Alpha department. "...the Alpha

Course is proving to be a most profitable vehicle for Rome's ecumenical goals." *(Alpha, the Unofficial Guide*, p. 55. Calvary Contender, March 2004.)

Catholic Alpha Centres are spread around the whole world. The Centre in The Hague, the Netherlands, recommends the course as a valuable instrument for the Church of this time. The holy Thérèse is the patron saint of Mission and Church teacher of God's merciful Love. The Alpha course is dedicated to her special intercession and help. (Katholiek Alpha Centrum, *Alpha cursus: kennismaken met het christelijk geloof.*)

The influence and result of Alpha should not be underestimated. We read that the *Alpha fever,*

> ...will inch its adherents inexorably closer to the Roman Catholic church. Rome has welcomed the courses, and waits with consummate patience to embrace those who wander from the path of Scripture... (*Evangelical Times, Alpha Courses and Catholicism.*)

Ambrose Griffiths, Roman Catholic bishop of Hexham and Newcastle, England, says that Alpha, "doesn't contain anything that is contrary to Catholic doctrine." (Paul Fitton, *The Alpha Course: It is Bible-Based or Hell-Inspired?* Part 2.)

Cardinal William Keeler of Baltimore has nothing but praise about Alpha.

> ...those who complete the Alpha course are ready and eager to take part in the small communities that are forming in parishes—ready and eager to learn more about our church and her sacraments and to serve and evangelise others. (*Alpha News International*, Aug-Nov. 1999.)

New Zealand's, Archbishop of Wellington, Cardinal Thomas Williams, opened an Alpha conference in July 1997, saying, "News of Alpha has been spreading fast and many churches—my own included—are becoming eager to learn more of its content and method, and of what Alpha might do in energising the life and mission of our parishes." After the conference Bishop John Dew declared in his diocesan newspaper, "Both Cardinal Tom and I would be very happy to see Alpha used within the Catholic Church." (*News Archive,* uk.alpha.

org. 1999.)

Another source writes:

> Alpha has heavy connections to the global Anglican Church, which is united very strongly with the political might of the United Nations; and Alpha is heavily involved with the Vatican's political might as well! (Wendy Howard, Endtime Ministries, Christian Research Centre, *Dialectic, Praxis and the Alpha Course*, p. 5.)

Nicky Gumbel, the author of Alpha, says that it is an exciting thing that God breaks down church walls these days. People don't care much

> ...whether you are a Methodist or a Baptist, whether you are a Roman Catholic or an Anglican. These are not the significant things...There is only one body...So it doesn't matter whether you are a Roman Catholic or a Protestant.

Nicky then tells about a Baptist minister whom he says thinks his church is the true one and that he didn't want to take part in an ecumenical effort. Nicky calls this pastor a

> ...very, very bigoted and arrogant man...it is a very unusual attitude these days because most people recognize that the Spirit of God unites us with...every denomination, because there is one family... (Elizabeth McDonald & Dusty Peterson, *Alpha, the Unofficial Guide*, St Matthew Publ., Ltd, Cambridge, 2004, pp. 52, 53.)

Everyone is supposed to take part in the Ecumenical Movement and those who find it difficult to go along with its principles are regarded as loveless conservatives and extremists who spoil the progress of Christian unity and often they are accused and derided. Is it really worth it to stay apart?

Sadler declares:

> ...the Ecumenical Movement is a 'world' movement. It is about creating a one-world government and religion, and is another version of the New World Order of the Occult. Just like with Freemasonry, the ordinary followers of the Ecumenical Movement have no idea of the movement's true aims and sinister connections. It is dressed up in a façade of Christianity, so as to deceive. (I. A. Sadler, *Mystery, Babylon the Great*, Reprint 2003, p. 244.)

Unity in diversity is the popular motto. It tries to unite people from all kinds of religions in one huge world church. Unity in diversity was the motto of the Amsterdam conference in 2000 with 10.000 church leaders present from 209 countries. The BWA (Baptist World Alliance) which believes unity is more important than doctrinal truth and which supports New Age One-World organizations such as the United Nations, was also present. (Cathy Burns, *Billy Graham and his Friends*, p. 482.)

Alpha also aims clearly at this same goal:

> Being involved with Alpha will bring the church-goer into a full blown ecumenical movement which is rapidly heading down the One World Church trail, under the Vatican and the United Nations. There is no way that the Alpha organization will avoid full inclusion into the politically-motivated One World and its government, it cannot because it is already so far advanced into the NWO. When people are moving along with Alpha, feel so much a part of it, revere such leaders as Nicky Gumbel, they will move easily and happily into the next step—UNION within Christendom and with non-Christian religious groups...The New Age experience-orientated global religiosity will be seen as merely another example of a search for God. (Howard, *The Alpha Course,* p.17.)

It is noteworthy that there is a pyramid shaped mystical meditation room in the UN building, which was redecorated by the late UN secretary general Dag Hammarskjold. There are occult symbols; characteristics of Freemasonry and in the middle of the room stands a big black altar block of stone. * World leaders and Illuminati masterminds come to meditate in that room. Robert Muller, member of the New Age and former assistant secretary general said:

> We must move as quickly as possible to a one-world government; a one-world religion; under a one-world leader...My great personal dream is to get a tremendous alliance between all major religions and the UN. (Cathy Burns, *Billy Graham and his Friends,* pp. 130, 131.)

> * There's a lot of power in those symbols. Putting up those symbols is an admission that you would like to have devil powers around. (T. E. Wade, *Spirit Possession*, Gazelle Publ., 1991, p. 59.)

Chapter 30

Meditation

The New Age movement aims at global religious unity and this has caused her not only to promote Eastern religions in Western countries, but also to introduce New Age thinking into as many areas of social life as possible, including the Churches.

Meditation, as a form of "contemplative spirituality" or "spiritual formation" plays a very important and distinctive role in the New Age movement. As attractively wrapped in biblical terms, it subtly entices and wins Christians to occult concepts and practices. This must not be underestimated. This invasive belief system is promoted by many church-growth leaders and has infected the church from the Alpha Course to the Purpose Driven Life and Seeker Sensitive services. It is the bridge that leads to interspirituality and unites all world's religions. Research Centre "Lighthouse Trails" presented the following alarming reports:

> Meditative practices are showing up everywhere. From Yoga to Reiki to contemplative and centering prayer, from breath prayers, the Jesus prayer, labyrinths, and Taize worship...meditation has greatly impacted our whole society. Interspiritual mystics proclaim that the people of the world will someday come together and realize they are all one with each other and with God, and they will accomplish this *realization of unity* through meditation. Unfortunately, this unity will not conform to the biblical foundation of unity, which is the preaching of the Cross. (*Lighthouse Trails Research Newsletter*, June 11, 2006.)

2005 was a very eventful year for the church as **contemplative spirituality gained momentum and has literally swept into**

churches, colleges, organizations and ministries at an astronomical rate. From Purpose Driven to the emerging church movement, from once respected Christian leaders to publishing companies and nearly every denomination, few stones have been left unturned... contemplative spirituality is here. (Ibid., January/February 2006. Emphasis added.)

Since so many Christians readily accept "contemplative spirituality" and earnestly believe that by its disciplines "the presence of God" is experienced, is it not rather undesirable then to question this "spiritual formation movement"? But does this kind of spirituality really bring us closer to God and to His Word? Perhaps the answer could be best given by a strong proponent of this spirituality. The noted Sue Monk Kidd, once a conservative Baptist, became firmly rooted in contemplative spirituality. Consider her testimony in one of her books:

> The minister was preaching. He was holding up a Bible...He was saying that the Bible was the sole and ultimate authority of the Christian's life...I remember a feeling rising up...a passionate, determined feeling, and it spread out from the core of me like a current...It was the purest inner knowing I had experienced, and it was shouting in me *no, no, no!* The ultimate authority of my life is not the Bible; it is not confined between the covers of a book. It is not something written by men and frozen in time. It is not from a source outside myself. *My ultimate authority is the divine voice in my own soul.* Period. (Sue Monk Kidd, *The Dance of the Dissident Daughter,* San Francisco, Harper Collins, 1996, p. 76.)

To every sincere Christian this testimony is really alarming. **If the inner divine voice of the own soul is more valued than the voice of God's holy Word and when the Bible as the sole and ultimate authority of man's life is denied or down-graded, then we can be sure that this kind of contemplative spirituality is the work of evil spirits.**

We can whole-heartedly agree with the words written in the *Lighthouse Newsletter:*

> The Bible says that in latter times seducing spirits will deceive great numbers of people. May the Lord help us to maintain the integrity of the gospel message of Jesus Christ, and may each believer be given strength and wisdom to speak the truth in love to a world

rushing headlong into darkness. (June 11, 2006.)

The Interspirituality of the Contemplative Movement equally values all religions. Christian beliefs have no preferences above other religious convictions. Christ is not the only way, nor the only truth and the life. No, He is just one among others. Consider how the exclusive God is judged and how personal holiness is possible outside Christianity:

> The exclusivist god is narrow, rigid, and blind. This god pays no attention to the sanctity and personal holiness of people outside the Christian fold. This god takes no loving and parental pride in the lives of great spiritual teachers who spoke of other paths to truth, figures like Moses, Siddartha, Mohammed, and Gandhi...Such a god is not worthy of honour, glory, worship, or praise. (Michael Ingham, *Mansions of the Spirit,* Anglican Book Centre, 1997, p. 61.)

This sinister statement should wake up every true Christian since the Bible clearly teaches that there is no God besides the King and Redeemer of Israel and no one can ever sanctify himself or attain holiness without being born again by God's power. Man's righteous deeds are like a filthy rag. (1 Sam. 2:2. Isa. 44:6, 7; 64:6. Jer. 13:23. Eph. 4:24. 1 Thess. 5:23. Heb. 13:12.)

Let us carefully explore this important subject further. Note how the introduction into the Christian churches of New Age concepts and meditation as a special target is part of the agenda of the New Age Mastermind.

Will Baron, as a former New Age priest,

> ...was seduced into becoming part of a secret invasion force of counterfeit Christians. As he subtly introduced his listeners to New Age concepts packaged in Christian terminology, he sincerely believed he was working for the Jesus Christ of the Bible.

> His incredible experience reveals the deceptive workings of the New Age master plan to infiltrate the body of Christ. The grand finale of the plan is predicted to be the appearance of the Antichrist in the church amidst a display of incredible signs, wonders, and miracles. From bitter experience, **Will regards the deception to be far more powerful and dangerous than most people realize.**

Meditation • 131

> **The Mastermind's agents may have infiltrated into your own church, and you are not aware of who they are. They are not easy to recognize because they seem to talk and behave like normal Christians."** (*Deceived by the New Age,* Pacific Press, 1990, Introduction, p. 8. Emphasis added.)

It is really alarming that Rick Warren's books, as well as other church-growth literature, hide New Age features including meditative practices. Even more serious is its wide acceptance by the churches. Will Baron, explains:

> I was also told to attend regular Christian church congregations so that I could meet new friends and interest them in meditation and other less offensive New Age ideas disguised in biblical-sounding terms. Avoiding anything too controversial, I presented subtle suggestions here and there. I found quite a few people who were willing to listen to my interesting proposals... (*Deceived by the New Age,* p. 11.)

He further testifies:

> **Knowledge, success, and oneness with 'God'** are the promises the New Age movement presents to the potential victims it is about to ensnare. And thousands of unsuspecting individuals—Christians and atheists alike—are swallowing this lure. Many orthodox Christians, including some pastors, have tasted the New Age bait and found that it 'was good for food and pleasing to the eye, and also desirable for gaining wisdom' (Genesis 3:6). (Ibid., p. 13. Emphasis added.)

Continuing, Baron warns:

> If you have desired to seek closeness with God, perhaps meditation has attracted your attention, that so-called science of seeking communion with God. You may have wondered whether it is really a good idea for a Christian to meditate. I first began to practice New Age introspective meditation in a class at the Lighted Way metaphysical center. Some people begin New Age meditation techniques right in their own churches...This type of introspective meditation is not found in the Bible, and it has never been part of orthodox Christian activity. It is a Hindu practice that is undesirable and potentially dangerous! (Ibid., pp. 14, 15.)

The answer to Baron's question in the first part of the above quote is: Yes, indeed, it is "a good idea for a Christian to meditate." The vital question, however, is, what are the principles of true meditation? The most sinister heresies are based upon counterfeits of the most important principles.

The very "secret infiltration" Baron describes below is enough to recognize that the deceiver of Eden is behind this kind of meditation. "Communion with god" must thus be spelled with a little "g," for only the "god of this world" uses deception in seeking communion with Christians.

In Chapter 13, "Secret Infiltration," Baron specifically tells that a new mission project was assigned to him:

> I was to secretly infiltrate a local Christian church… My task was to search for suitable contacts and make friends with them. Then I was to subtly introduce them to the concept of Christian meditation as a means of communion with God. The ultimate goal was to start a meditation group within the congregation. (Ibid., p. 170.)

In stressing the cunning role that meditation or the contemplative prayer movement plays, Baron declares:

> Meditation provides an excellent opportunity for Satan to exercise his manipulating deception. Why else would New Agers be promoting it so heavily? (Ibid., p. 200.)

Ray Yungen justly appeals:

> I challenge the Christian community to look at the facts surrounding the contemplative prayer movement and see its connection to New Age occultism and Eastern mysticism…After taking an honest look at the evidence, the conclusion is overwhelming that contemplative prayer is not a spiritually-sound practice for Christians. (*A Time of Departing,* 2nd Ed., 2006, Lighthouse Trails Publ., Silverton, Oregon, pp. 89, 130.)

As we have seen a few paragraphs before, Will Baron identifies three "states that the New Age promises": **knowledge, success,** and **oneness with God.**

This is most significant, for these echo the promises of Eden's serpent. Don't be deceived by "Oneness with God." For this is none other than the New Ager, pantheistic god, of which we are presumed to be a part. Thus the real meaning is, "Ye shall be gods, knowing good and evil—a promise of ultimate success, which climaxes continual successes.

It is remarkable and no accident that Rick Warren in his book both highlights meditation and promises: knowledge, success, and unity with God. Indeed, he assures that if you study his book, a "40-day spiritual journey," you will receive **knowledge** as to "God's purpose for your life" and you will **know** what on earth you are here for and how to live in **oneness with God** a **successful** and purpose driven life. Constant conversation; continual **meditation** and also the discovery of your Shape, are central themes in Warren's book. Although he uses prayer and meditation to present this so that it appears biblical, his methods come directly from New Age instructions.

Warren makes clear in his book, that there should be **constant conversation** and **continual meditation**.

> You can carry on a continuous, open-ended conversation with him throughout your day, talking with him about whatever you are doing or thinking at that moment. 'Praying without ceasing' means conversing with God while shopping, driving, working, or performing any other every day tasks. (*The Purpose Driven Life,* pp. 87, 88.)

Such statements appear to represent bible truth. But a primary satanic strategy is to lead God's people into careless neglect both of Christian privileges and of vital principles of truth and then raise someone up to appear to emphasize these, but who actually introduces a counterfeit to promote sinister heresies.

Thus, despite its use of true and vital expressions, the above statement is designed to lead us away from that which the words appear to convey. But, yes, indeed, not only should more time be devoted to prayer than is usual, but we should always maintain continual spiritual connection with God.

E. G. White writes:

> As the body is continually receiving the nourishment that sustains life and vigor, so the soul must be constantly communing with Christ, submitting to Him and depending wholly upon Him. (*Thoughts From The Mount of Blessing,* p. 19.)

But she also explains:

> The Saviour has told us to pray without ceasing. The Christian can not always be in the position of prayer, but his thoughts and desires can always be upward. (*Sons and Daughters of God,* p. 99.)

Though we can not always be in a position of prayer, Ellen White insists that our thoughts and desires can always be attuned to heaven in a submissive way to Christ, depending wholly upon Him. God wants our minds to be always directed by His Spirit and this can be true when making personal decisions; doing math or business, or performing any other task. Thus, we should never forget our regular contact with God whatever the many daily cares, worries and agitations.

"The church needs the fresh, living experience of members who have habitual communion with God." (*Christian Service,* p. 212.) To maintain this we are counseled, moreover, to have set times for Bible study and prayer every day and also to have special times for intercessory prayer.

> Jesus, when preparing for some great trial or some important work, would resort to the solitude of the mountains and spend the night in prayer to His Father...We, too, must have times set apart for meditation and prayer and for receiving spiritual refreshing. (*The Ministry of Healing,* p. 509.)

The difference between Warren's teaching and Ellen White's regarding meditation and continual communion will become increasingly evident in the next section, as we see clear evidences that his method is directly contrary to the principles of God's Word. Meanwhile, a few statements below illustrate that the life of a Christian should be well-balanced with a time to work, a time to rest and recreate and a time to pray and meditate:

> The Christian life is not made up of unceasing activity, or of continual meditation. Christians must work earnestly for the salvation of the lost, and they must also take time for contemplation, for prayer, and the study of the Word of God. It will not do to be always under the strain of the work and excitement, for in this way personal piety is neglected, and the powers of mind and body are injured... All who are under the training of God need the quiet hour for communion with their own hearts, with nature, and with God. (*Christian Service,* p. 249.)

We must take periods of rest, periods of recreation and periods for contemplation. (*My Life Today*, p. 214.)

We are not to spend our time wholly in prayerful meditation, neither are we to drive and hurry and work as if this were required in order that we should gain heaven, while neglecting to devote time to the cultivation of personal piety. (*Our High Calling*, p. 221.)

On January 7 and 13, 2011, Rick Warren announced on his website the launch of the Daniel Plan. A plan in which Medical professionals will share how to get healthy for life.

Rick Warren writes: "I can't tell you how excited I am about the Decade of Destiny and what's coming up at Saddleback. Next weekend, we're launching the Daniel Plan, a 52-week plan to help you become physically healthier." He calls the Daniel plan *God's Prescription For Your Health* and invites: "Be a part of this transformational debut to be a healthier you!"
(http://saddleback.com/blogs/newsandviews/news--views-1711/)

Introducing the Daniel plan this way, makes it sound innocent, exciting and attractive. However, the three doctors who developed the program, Mehmet Oz, Daniel Amen and Mark Hyman, are strong advocates of Eastern mystical practices.

Dr. Mehmet Oz, stated in his broadcast talk show (Ultimate Alternative Medicine Secrets) of January 6, 2010: "Try Reiki... Reiki is one of my favourites, we've been using it for years in the Oz family, and we swear by it."

Dr. Oz's wife, Lisa, is a Reiki Master. The Oz couple hold Reiki workshops and teach Hatsurei Ho meditation, which is "possibly the most effective way to increase the depth, quality and intensity of ones connection to the Reiki phenomenon."
(http://www.aetw.org/d_hatsurei_ho.html)

Reiki is a form of New Age Chakra energy healing. A chakra is one of seven basic centres in the body with dormant energy, or kundalini power, at the base of the spine. Through meditation this mystic energy will be awakened, activating each chakra with its specific function and level of awareness. This process is seen as being healthy, enhancing life and curing maladies. However, this process brings people into

contact with the occult spirit world. Spiritual astral guides assist in the healing process and may prefer to stay always with you.
(http://www.youtube.com/watch?v=l4N2URu4avY)

His colleague, Dr. Daniel Amen, is a Tantric sex promoter. He teaches brain health, and includes meditation. His instructor was the mystic Tantra educator T. J. Bartel. Dr. Amen wrote:

> In my book The Brain in Love, I wrote about Tantric sexual practices, and was fascinated by the concept, which involves using the mind - the brain, that is - to enhance sexual response and intimacy. I wanted to experience it for myself... Finding someone... took quite a bit of research. In the end, T J Bartel, an advanced certified Tantra educator, became our teacher. Our experience with him was amazing and transformative... TJ was such a wonderful teacher that I felt as if I had to share his knowledge with everyone I knew. (*Change Your Brain, Change Your Body*, p. 283.)

This union of sexuality and mystic spirituality indicates or represents a union with the divine. As a recommended popular ancient tool for healing, it illustrates how much ancient Eastern practices and New Age thinking has penetrated our modern society.

In another book, *Making a Good Brain Great*, Dr. Amen writes: "I recommend an active form of yoga meditation called Kriya Kirtan. It is based on the five primal sounds saa, taa, naa, maa, aa." (p. 238.) And the advice is that these sounds should be repeated for 12 minutes straight.

The Kriya Kirtan that he speaks about is a form of kundalini yoga. When this is practiced during meditation a special force is activated. This kundalini force, or the divine, serpent power, is then awakened and it will travel up the spine as a mystical current and create a feeling of being divine. (See Appendix II for more information about the many possible kundalini effects).

Dr. Mark Hyman, the third medical professional in the Daniel Plan, recommends various mystic ancient tools. He emphasizes:

> You have to learn tools to actively relax such as meditation, yoga, deep breathing, hypnosis... The Tibetan monks used meditation, which is very easy to learn... Mindfulness meditation is a powerful well-researched tool, developed by Buddhists, but now prac-

ticed and used all over the world... Pray, chant, dance and celebrate. All these are ancient tools for healing... Practice tai qi quan or qi gong. These are ancient, energy balancing tools..." (*The Ultramind Solution*, pp. 59, 278, 384.)

These 'Tai qi quan or qi gong' are internal styles of Chinese martial art and refer to the ancient Chinese cosmological concept of the two opposite forces Yin and Yang as being the foundation of creation. (http://www.shenwu.com/taichi.htm)

This Daniel Plan (also called Orange County Health & Fitness Seminar) with the involvement of these three doctors, illustrates again how deeply Rick Warren and his Saddleback church are involved in ancient spiritistic practices and disciplines.

Ellen White aptly noted: "The line of distinction between professed Christians and the ungodly is now hardly distinguishable... Satan determines to unite them... by sweeping all into the ranks of spiritualism... Papists, Protestants, and worldlings... will see in the union a grand movement for the conversion of the world and the ushering in of the long expected millennium. Through spiritualism, Satan appears as a benefactor of the race, healing the diseases of the people, and professing to present a new and more exalted system of religious faith; but at the same time he works as a destroyer. His temptations are leading multitudes to ruin." (*The Great Controversy*, pp. 588, 589.)

Chapter 31

'Breath Prayers'

As we examine Warren's recommendation of "breath prayers," we will see that what he presents as Scriptural is a New Age method that violates Scripture. Note how his over-literal interpretation actually denies the Bible principle involved, even while directly contradicting Christ's own instruction:

Quoting the *Message Bible* Warren writes: "The Bible tells us to 'pray all the time.'" He then explains how to put this into practice:

> How is it possible to do this? O\ne way is to use 'breath prayers' throughout the day, as many Christians have done for centuries. You choose a brief sentence or a simple phrase that can be repeated to Jesus in one breath: 'You are with me.' 'I receive your grace.' 'I'm depending on you.' 'I want to know you.' 'I belong to you.' 'Help me trust you.' You can also use a short phrase of Scripture: 'For me to live is Christ.' 'You will never leave me.' 'You are my God.' Pray it as often as possible so it is rooted deep in your heart...(*The Purpose Driven Life,* p. 89.)

To discern the distortion of Bible truth we need to consider that while the Bible may be distorted by spiritualizing it away, it may be as seriously distorted by over-literalizing. Indeed, though opposite, these generally go together, with one being dominant and the other a necessary tool of that domination. Over-literalizing is especially dangerous, as it appears to be conscientious application, but in reality violates the principle involved. Thus, some have violated Christ's message: "If your eye offends you pluck it out," by taking it literally. Christ was not talking about literal eyes or hands, but spiritual issues of commitment. Such over-literalizing seriously violates God's Word by obscuring and belittling the spiritual principles involved.

Breath prayers Warren suggests to fulfill the Bible injunction to "pray all the time" are based on a poor translation that tends to over-literalizing Paul's admonition to "pray without ceasing." True prayer involves meaningful communion with God, not merely a rote repetition of a phrase. In true prayer, what is said is not the all important thing, but a heart uplifted to God in true petition, gratitude and/or praise. Warren's expressions would all be good in appropriate individual communion with the mind focused on Christ. But even "You are my God" is meaningless when it becomes rote, as is instructed. Like the rosary, such repetitious expression is a key to self-hypnosis, a method used by New Agers who advocate meaningless syllables, such as are used to induce tongue speaking—which originated in Paganism.

Prayer at its best involves conversation with God in which we listen much of the time to the things He will speak to us. Says Ellen White: "Our prayers will take the form of a conversation with God as we would talk with a friend. He will speak His mysteries to us personally." (*Lift Him Up*, p. 113.)

This kind of communication, in a way, can be likened to a husband and wife as being each other's best earthly friends who work together, eat together, and relax together through the day. They talk to each other, but often relate to each other without words as they deal with various issues. From time to time they discuss things or plan together, always consulting together before making key decisions. Imagine when over and over again the same things are said, would that enhance or hinder communication?

God is no more pleased with a continuous stream of rote utterances than would a husband or wife appreciate a stream of rote utterances on the part of the other.

Indeed, this would effectively block all real communication, which is the purpose in heathen worship—to prevent true communication with God and to empty the mind for demon control. This was one of Satan's great triumphs in the time of Christ, concerning which He specifically warned in His kingdom of heaven sermon known as the "sermon on the mount." In teaching how not to pray, He admonished: "But when you pray, do not use vain repetitions as the heathen do."

(Mt. 6:7; NKJV.)

Consider Warren's following admonition:

> Practicing the presence of God is a skill, a habit you can develop. Just as musicians practice scales every day in order to play beautiful music with ease, you must force yourself to think about God at different times in your day. You must train your mind to remember God. At first you will need to create reminders to regularly bring your thoughts back to the awareness that God is with you in that moment. Begin by placing visual reminders around you. You might post little notes that say, 'God is with me and for me right now! (*The Purpose Driven Life*, p. 89.)

This may sound good. But whose power is directing? Is this the same counsel as that given by Ellen White? Or are there clear contrasts? Let us note a statement that verbally appears to express the same thing as does Warren:

> Cultivate the habit of talking with the Saviour when you are alone, when you are walking and when you are busy with your daily labor. Let the heart be continually uplifted in silent petition for help, for light, for strength, for knowledge. Let every breath be a prayer. (*Ministry of Healing*, p. 511.)

What is said is important. More important is what is meant. To understand what Warren meant we need to examine his explanations and the context, as we do here. To understand Ellen White's meaning we must examine her various explanations along with the context. And in doing so we find that the meaning is as contrary to Warren's as the words are parallel. For Ellen White consistently emphasizes the importance to truth and testing the spirits, whereas Warren specifically warns against such attempts. Moreover, while the purpose of Warren's Eastern meditation is to empty the mind by rote repetition, she emphasizes the importance of filling the mind with Scripture and focusing upon the person of Christ as He ministers in the Most Holy Place.

The true Spirit does not ask us to empty our minds, but to fill them with the truth of Scripture. Christ was, as our example to follow, so filled with Scripture that His every response to temptation was a *Thus saith the Lord*. "Only by the word could He resist temptation." (*The Desire of Ages*, p. 123.)

When, however, we empty the mind and silence our thoughts, we are actually blocking out God's Word and resisting His Spirit Who directs by means of the very principles we are silencing. Thus we become a defenceless prey without the power of the Holy Spirit and His Word. How then can we follow our Lord's example and overcome temptation?

We are admonished:

> When assailed by temptation, look not to circumstances or to the weakness of self, but to the power of the word. All its strength is yours. (Ibid., p. 123.)

To justify their contemplative disciplines of emptying and silencing the mind some refer to the words in Psalms 46:10, "Be still and know that I am God." The preceding verses, however, describe the mighty works of God showing His greatness, power and sovereignty. This, and not any mystic practice, is the basis for being at rest; trusting God and in no wise murmuring, objecting or opposing but calmly and humbly submitting to Him. This Bible passage in no way sanctions contemplative disciplines of silencing the mind. There is no evidence here whatsoever that vindicates Eastern practices of entering a state of trance or altered state of consciousness. No, the Bible nowhere approves of such mystic activities.

Warren suggests to practice the presence of God, even with all kinds of reminders hanging around, to force contact with God and to repeat on the rhythm of our breathing, again and again a short prayer.

But where did Warren get his ideas? From the Bible? Warren tells us:

> The classic book on learning how to develop a constant conversation with God is *'Practicing the Presence of God.'* It was written in the seventeenth century by Brother Lawrence, a humble cook in a French monastery. (*The Purpose Driven Life,* p. 88.)

Who is this Brother Lawrence?

It is remarkable to read that when something had taken this devout Brother Lawrence's mind away from thinking of God he would receive a reminder from Him that so moved his soul "that he cried out, singing and dancing violently like a madman." (Brother Lawrence,

The Practice of the Presence of God, translated by John Delaney, Image Books, 1977, Third Conversation, p. 34 or other edition pp. 46, 47.)

This deportment is peculiar for a real Christian and does not seem to indicate true spiritual maturity. It is rather more indicative of phenomena in Eastern religious mysticism.

Richard Bennett, a former priest, tells us that,

> Brother Lawrence was not only traditionally Roman Catholic but also disseminated teachings that have similarities with Hinduism in the Bhagavad-Gita, and with many New Age writers. (Brian Flynn, *Running Against the Wind,* Lighthouse Trails Publ., Silverton, Oregon, Second ed., 2005, p. 199.)

This mystical source with New Age Eastern religious leanings is not a very acceptable source for sincere Christians to learn how to pray and meditate, and have a constant conversation with God.

The source of Warren's stress on the importance of short prayers is the pantheistic concept that God is everywhere and in everything. This becomes evident to discerning readers in his following statement:

> Because God is with you all the time, no place is any closer to God than the place where you are right now. The Bible says, 'He rules everything and is everywhere and is in everything.' Another of Brother Lawrence's helpful ideas was to pray shorter conversational prayers continually through the day rather than trying to pray long sessions of complex prayers. (*The Purpose Driven Life,* p. 88.)

God indeed rules everything and by His Spirit is always with us. But the idea that "He is in everything" comes straight from the pantheistic philosophy Dr. Kellogg sought to introduce within Adventism a century ago.

On the next page Warren recommends the habit of certain monks. "Benedictine monks use the hourly chimes of a clock to remind them to pause and pray 'the hour prayer.' If you have a watch or cell phone with an alarm, you could do the same." (Ibid., p. 89.)

Sounds innocent? Yes, indeed. Counterfeits are designed to appear innocent. But the forms of prayer and meditation that Warren and many other leaders advocate are enveloped by a mystic

New Age sphere. **Especially the "breath prayers" carry the typical characteristics of Eastern religions.**

In what appears to be a sweeping phenomenon, Rick Warren and other Christian leaders are embracing practices and a new spirituality that borrows from Eastern mysticism and New Age philosophy. The changes are taking place worldwide and involve many of the most popular evangelical leaders including Rick Warren, Brian McLaren, Richard Foster, Tony Campolo, and Eugene Peterson. In Rick Warren's *Purpose-Driven Life*, on Day Eleven, he encourages people to practice "breath prayers" by repeating words and phrases over and over in a mantra-style prayer, a practice used centuries ago by a group of mystical monks known as the Desert Fathers. This so-called "prayer" is identical to that found in Hindu yoga and Zen Buddhism. (Lighthouse Trails Research Project, March 24, 2005; (Reviews) *Rick Warren and Other Leaders Promoting New Age*, March 27, 2005.)

Some may wonder if we are not making a mountain of a mole hill. Does Rick Warren really have close ties with unchristian New Age Eastern religious practices? Or are there just surface similarities? For there appear to be striking similarities to Bible teaching.

Warren himself in various ways answers this question. One way is by his favourable preface in *The Emerging Church*, a book written by Dan Kimball, promoting also New Age meditation techniques of Oriental origin.

He also recommends the book *Serious Times* by James Emery White. The book is filled with contemplative references including numerous mentions of Thomas Merton, Richard Foster, the Desert Fathers etc. The book encourages the mystical use of "lectio divina" and the silence to enhance spiritual life. (Warren's *weekly e-newsletter,* January 18, 2006. Ministry Library Section.)

Nor did Warren hesitate to speak on the "National Pastor's Convention" in 2004 "right after a workshop on Yoga, which happened to follow a labyrinth and contemplative prayer exercises." (*Lighthouse Newsletter*, March, 2005; Cf., Jan. 5, 2005.)

And indeed, Rick Warren spoke during the "Aspen's Ideas Festival" on July 5th–10th at the "Aspen Institute" along with New Agers, contemplatives, Buddhists, homosexuals, and others. (Cf., *Lighthouse*

Newsletter, July, 2005.)

That Warren doesn't shun occult prayer practices was also very clear when he, in 1997, took part, as a prominent speaker, in Yonggi Cho's Church Growth Conference. Cho is a follower of occult ideas and known to mix occult concepts with Christian teaching. (Cf., *Community Connections*, Let Us Reason Ministries, P.O. Box 860683, Wahiawa HI 96786.)

Cho became known by his mystical visualization-techniques and Robert Schuller wrote in the foreword to Cho's book *The Fourth Dimension*,

> I discovered the reality of that dynamic dimension in prayer that comes through visualizing....Don't try to understand it. Just start to enjoy it! It's true. It works. I tried it.

Cho writes in his book:

> If Buddhists and Yoga practitioners can accomplish their objectives through fourth dimensional powers, then Christians should be able to accomplish much more by using the same means. (Paul Yonggi Cho, *The Fourth Dimension*, vol. 1, 1979, pp. 37, 41.)

Cho even writes blasphemously in the same book:

> You create the presence of Jesus with your mouth...He is bound by your lips and by your words...Remember that Christ is depending upon you and your spoken word to release His presence. (Ibid., p. 83.)

In his interview with Cho, Warren spoke not a single critical word. Nor did he reveal any form of aloofness. Instead he revealed only feelings of respect and esteem and he asked Cho: "Can you please pray a prayer of blessing to the pastors that are reading this?" (*Community Connections*, Let Us Reason Ministries.)

Is it any wonder that Warren introduces Oriental prayer techniques and mystical "breath prayers" in his book *The Purpose Driven Life?* He certainly walks on slippery ground. But notwithstanding its occult origin, these repetitive "breath prayers" are introduced into many churches and increasingly practiced.

"Youth Ministry," for instance, shows a picture of teenagers, some sitting down and others walking a single path, called "the labyrinth," while chanting repetitive breath prayers.

The technique of these prayers is described as follows:

> Sit quietly and repeat the phrase gently in your mind for several minutes. Allow the prayer to take on the shape of your breathing so that the words accompany your every breath. Take a walk, repeating your prayer while you move. Note how the prayer shapes your perceptions. Allow the prayer to accompany the rhythm of your walking and your breathing…Always, the tools of contemplative prayer are used only to help guide us to an experience of union with God. In the temporal moment of contemplative prayer we are drawn even momentarily into the eternal realm that transcends our time. (*Presbyterian Church, Youth Ministry, Spirituality, Prayers*, April 20, 2004, pp 1, 3.)

"[I]nto the eternal realm that transcends our time" is a new age expression. And the method advocated is designed to induce a form of self-hypnosis, which **removes reason and will** and prepares one to become the subject of "wicked spirits in high places."

To Warren's recommendation of this kind of mystical prayers Mac Dominick comments as follows:

> While this may appear to be very spiritual, a quick review of occult New Age magazines and newsletters show these very labyrinths and speak of attaining the altered states of consciousness via transcendental meditation (TM). TM is a technique utilized by those who wish to access 'spirit guides' in their 'safe place'. **Repetitive 'praying' and chanting originate in occult religions, and have no place in Christian practice.** There is absolutely no doubt of the occult nature of these methods when one realizes the significance of the statement, 'help guide us to an experience of union with God.' This is not a Christian concept, but rather, a Pantheistic principle. The believer will never be 'one with God' [We can only be at one with Him. We will forever be creatures, wholly dependent upon Him] Only Jesus Christ is or can be one with the Father. This teaching is based on eastern religion and occult teachings. Yet, this practice is on the web site of the Presbyterian Church USA website, and Rick Warren condones 'breath prayers' in his book, *The Purpose-driven Life*. Jesus Himself warned that Christians are not to pray with '**vain repetitions as the heathen do**' (Matt. 6:7) because He fully realized the extreme dangers involved in this practice. Yet Dr.

Warren advocates that which Jesus directly condemns. (Mac Dominick, *Outcome-Based Religion: Purpose, Apostasy, & The New Paradigm Church,* 2005, p. 301. Emphasis added.)

Mac Dominick here puts his finger on the real issue. While the Bible asks us to "pray without ceasing," the occult asks us to use "vain repetitions" a Pagan practice which Jesus forbids, that involves emptying the mind and substitutes for real communion with God.

Though Rick Warren recommends Christian words or biblical phrases, these practices, how-ever attractive they may appear, are very dangerous.

The one objective of contemplative prayer, breath prayers, mantra—and transcendental meditation, or whatever other appellation, is to seek super sensual contact with a higher power by creating an altered state of consciousness whereby the thoughts are brought to rest by repeating a keyword or a short phrase.

The "altered state of consciousness" sought represents a state of trance or hypnosis which permits evil spirits to control the mind, even placing within it ideas and commands to be acted upon later.

Burns explains:

> These 'words of power' are REPEATED OVER AND OVER again until this trance-like condition is achieved. In this state, the mind is opened to all kinds of demonic activity and influence because the person's rational, thinking ability has been set aside by the REPETITION of the words he or she has spoken. Is it any wonder that the Bible warns us not to use 'VAIN REPETITIONS, as the HEATHEN do…' (Matthew 6:7)? God knew that the use of repetitious words would open us up to demonic influence and, therefore, He warned us not to do this. In spite of biblical warning NOT to use REPETITIOUS words and phrases, so-called 'Christian' leaders (…) are now telling us to use a word or phrase OVER AND OVER again…" (Cathy Burns, *Billy Graham and His Friends,* Sharing, Mt. Carmel, PA, Second Printing, 2002, p. 506. Emphasis in original.)

Concerning this practice, Yungen declares:

> One gradually **tunes out his conscious thinking process** until an altered state of consciousness comes over him. (Ray Yungen, *For Many Shall Come In My Name,* Solid Rock Books, Revised Edition, Woodburn Oregon, 1991, p. 10. Emphasis added.)

'Breath Prayers' • 147

Bryan Flynn is right on in his analysis and conclusion:

> Breath prayer, in nearly every case, is used or described as a technique to silence the mind or supposedly to 'practice the presence.'...Breath prayers are just another way of using meaningless repetition to gain an altered state. The practitioners believe they will feel closer to God through this method...practicing the presence, breath prayers and contemplative prayer are mere **failures of faith** in the true Gospel, or ignorance of it, leading to delusion. (Brian Flynn, *Running Against the Wind,* Silverton, Oregon, 2005, pp. 199, 200. Emphasis added.)

Flynn earlier warns: "It is unbridled and **unprotected mental thought** that provides a perfect avenue for a demonic spirit world to intercept and redirect our way of thinking." (Ibid., p. 93. Emphasis added.)

Concerning the many church-growth leaders who teach and recommend in covert and guarded terms, breath prayers and mystical New Age eastern contemplative meditation Flynn declares:

> Willow Creek Community Church in Illinois has produced a number of contemplative authors and leaders, while the Willow Creek website boasts of a 'self-guided' 'contemplative worship service.' Ruth Haley Barton,...wrote the curriculum for teaching contemplative prayer at this church. More recently, she and John Ortberg, a former Willow Creek pastor, co-authored a book together. In this book, the reader is instructed to practice lectio divina, described by the authors as a slow meditative practice dating back to ancient times...Both Barton and Ortberg are promotors of the contemplative prayer movement, and both are featured speakers for the very contemplative National Pastor's Convention, hosted by Youth Specialties. This annual pastor's convention teaches yoga workshops and gives participants opportunity to walk through a labyrinth and attend contemplative prayer sessions. (Ibid., pp. 197, 198.)

Flynn continues,

> It is important to mention here that Willow Creek senior pastor, Bill Hybels, shares a speaking platform at the Willow Creek sponsored Leadership Summit conferences, with New Age sympathizer Ken Blanchard and Rick Warren...Thousands of churches, pastors, youth pastors, and other church leaders participate in Purpose-

Driven courses. If indeed contemplative prayer is being endorsed, promoted, and taught through Rick Warren, you can surmise that it will be coming to a church near you if it isn't there already, and the Purpose-Driven program will usher in contemplative prayer on an unprecedented scale...If Rick Warren's global peace plans are carried out, then the whole world will be introduced to mystical, mantra meditation... (Ibid., pp. 198, 200, 201.)

Flynn then questions,

> If Rick Warren is not a promotor of the contemplative prayer movement and all that this movement entails, why was he a featured speaker at the 2004 National Pastor's Convention which offered labyrinths, contemplative prayer sessions, and yoga? And why, in 2005, did Rick Warren invite contemplative leaders from Youth Specialties to give training at his Purpose Driven Youth Ministry conferences? (Ibid., p. 201.)

It is without doubt that Rick Warren and Bill Hybels as leaders of the most influential evangelical churches—Saddleback and Willow Creek—promote Eastern Meditation and the New Age.

At the Willow Creek Leadership Summit conference of August 10–12, 2006, attended by 70,000 Church leaders in 130 locations, one of the featured speakers, for instance, was Jim Collins who wrote a foreword in Michael Ray's book *The Highest Goal: The Secret That Sustains You in Every Minute.* (Berrett-Koehler, publishers, San Francisco, Ca, 2004/2005.)

Note that this book presents Eastern spirituality. It presents meditation techniques of emptying the mind and realizing the divinity within.

On page 28, for instance, the author relates his supernatural experience while attending an ashram—a Hindu spiritual center:

> "...I experienced an awakening, a new sense of the highest goal...As I sat in mediation...I suddenly felt and saw a bolt of lightning shoot up from the base of my spine out the top of my head. It forced me to recognize something great within me. And that recognition led to an experience of joy...this awareness of my own divinity."

Collins is trained in Eastern spirituality. He took Michael Ray's creativity course in 1982. The book of this course *Creativity in Business* reflects Eastern philosophy, mysticism and meditative practices and speaks about the effective use of Tarot cards (pp. 153, 154.) and how to "meet your wisdom-keeper or spirit-guide—an inner person who can be with you in life, someone to whom you can turn for guidance." (p. 37.)

In his foreword in Michael's book *The Highest Goal* Collins characterizes him "that he really is a yogi, as in a spiritual guide–leading us in meditation exercises." (p. xii.)

Can you imagine Jim Collins with his ties to mysticism and Eastern spirituality as a featured speaker at the Willow Creek conference attended by many thousands of Christian Church leaders?

Note how the "prompting" is described that made Hybels organize the "Leadership Summit" conferences: "Following a God-given prompting to raise the spiritual gift of leadership in and for the local church..." (Willow Creek website, *Leadership Summit 2006, Speakers: Bill Hybels.*)

Consider also how the 2006 conference was introduced:

> The Leadership Summit 2006 offers you and every leader on your team a place to rededicate yourselves to God's life-changing work. You'll be challenged to invest your gifts and abilities in the single most important work on this planet—helping your local church reach its full, God-given redemptive potential." (Ibid., *Leadership Summit 2006, Overview.*)

This sounds wonderful. But how can this ever be realized with featured speakers who are New Age sympathizers and promote Eastern Meditation techniques?

It cannot be denied that Satan is always ready to bring about a revival of feeling and he introduces with pleasure his extensive arsenal of mystical prayer practices, meditation techniques, popular music, and spiritual revival songs. These New Age songs, with frequent repetitions and with little variation, and often sung with drum beat accompaniment, are usually characterised by mystical expressions with words as: *fire, spirit, power, wind, hover, love, streaming, river, etc.,* wherewith the new spirituality is expressed.

By introducing these unbiblical prayer activities, meditation

techniques and spiritual revival songs into the church, stealthily and unnoticed a door will be opened for the influence of misleading demonic powers.

Chapter 32

Resisters

It won't be easy, but those who, in the light of God's Word, cannot agree with the popular developments that are taking place in the church, will at last find, when they remain faithful to God and His Word, that they have chosen the best part.

The desperate need for unity means that New Agers will do whatever is necessary to assimilate all Christians into their belief system, including calling the New Age religion 'Christianity', calling themselves 'Christians', and making their corrupt doctrine appear as biblical as possible. Any genuine Christian who refuses to join this unscriptural unification will **not** be tolerated by the false Church and will have to be converted **by force**. (McDonald & Dusty Peterson, *Alpha the unofficial guide,* Cambridge, 2004, p. 165. Emphasis added.)

We read with deep concern from a New Age source:

The new era is coming; the new ideals, the new civilization, the new modes of life, of education, of religious presentation and of government are slowly precipitating and naught can stop them. They can, however, be delayed by the reactionary types of people, by the ultra-conservative and closed minds, and by those who cling with adamantine determination to their beloved theories, their dreams and their visions, their interpretations and their peculiar and oft narrow understanding of the presented ideals. They are the ones who can and do hold back the hour of liberation. A spiritual fluidity, a willingness to let all preconceived ideas and ideals go, as well as all beloved tendencies, cultivated habits of thought and every determined effort to make the world conform to a pattern which seems to the individual the best because, to him, the most enticing—these must all be brought under the power of death. (Bailey, *The Exter-*

nalisation of the Hierarchy, pp. 278, 279.)

We are living in a time of transition! To be successful as well as appreciated in this new age depends on our ability and willingness to change. This modern transition movement has also affected the church. No wonder we are urged to leave "the old paths" behind. Traditional well-tried methods are now proclaimed to be outdated. New models and methods must be introduced. New forms of worship applied. Popular styles of music accepted. Modern ways of presentation utilized. A more up to date message preached. New truths and insights established. A new way of thinking stimulated. Yes, nearly all things must go differently than in the past. In short: a paradigm-shift must take place and everybody should eventually be forced to go along with this new mindset.

Of course, we should not be unwilling and narrow-minded to accept something new. Some changes are without doubt for the better. We should always be in for new methods and ways. But what if Bible principles are involved and violated? Does such a shift meet with God's approval? Will it ever be legitimate using violence to bring resisters in line?

> Christians are not to attempt to further the truth by violence. *False* believers, however, were only too happy to treat the Lord Jesus violently…and we have seen that *Rome's* spirit has frequently directed Catholics to do absolutely brutal things to those who choose to remain faithful to the whole of Scripture rather than submit to Rome's false ways and false leader… (McDonald & Peterson, *Alpha the unofficial guide,* p. 166.)

This spirit of intolerance, anger and sometimes even violence towards faithful Christians is also clearly seen in the modern church movements.

> …the spirit behind the 'Faith' movement has led its kingpins to rage against—and threaten—anyone who puts the Bible before 'Word-Faith' teachings. There are reports of 'stewards' at apostate church meetings angrily assaulting peaceful protestors, while those who speak out against apostasy are receiving hate-mail and even death threats from those they are trying to rescue. (Ibid.)

Since the Alpha, Toronto and Pensacola manifestations have affected many churches worldwide; and since these manifestations are identical with those seen in the Eastern mystic practice of Kundalini yoga, it is no wonder that in so many modern churches today a spirit of intolerant anger is revealed towards faithful believers.

> New Agers admit that the 'Kundalini' spirit can indeed cause 'seemingly unprovoked or excessive episodes of...rage.' (Ibid.)

If the manifested spirit behind Alpha and the modern revival movement is identical with the occult Kundalini spirit, then we should expect to find some similar evidence of anger or at least some threathening undercurrent.

And indeed, Alpha News (#13, p. 9.), for example, provides some clear evidence. We read: "Part of the Course was the Holy Spirit weekend...[My group was] being powerfully touched by the Spirit **and I began to feel angry.**" (Ibid. Emphasis added.)

This is not the fruit of God's Spirit. (Gal. 5:22.) "It is the dragon that is wroth; it is the spirit of satan that is revealed in anger and accusing." (E. G. White, *Desire of Ages,* p. 353.)

McDonald and Peterson confirm,

> We have found a real spirit of rage (as well as a spirit of confusion) among those who have received the T/P [Toronto/Pensacola] 'anointing' dispensed by Alpha...Indeed, a document partly written by HTB [Holy Trinity Brompton—Alpha's mother church] on how to behave when the 'Toronto Blessing' is ever questioned, actually has to warn against showing the anger that will frequently arise... (Ibid., pp. 166, 167.)

We may assume that satan with his cunning ways of deception has some ability to keep the spirit of anger below the surface and only activate it in his victims when it suits him.

It is according to Bible prophecy that, "in the last days perilous times shall come." The deceived will be "false accusers, incontinent, fierce, despisers of those that are good...Yea, and all that will live godly in Christ Jesus shall suffer persecution." (2 Tim. 3:1, 3, 12.)

There is even a special agenda how to bring believers in line with the new church-model and unite opponents in the religious unity of the universal spiritual New Age hierarchy.

To divert the churches from the old paths, (of preaching the Word and being familiar with Scripture) to the "Total Quality Management model" ways are to be found to bring opponents in line or otherwise rule them out. Berit Kjos, an able specialist, gives information for regular members, as to what is going on behind the scenes,—The hidden agenda. We read:

> The popular church management manual, *Leading Congregational Change* (LCC), promoted by Bob Buford's Leadership Network, offers a well-used plan. 'This is a book you ought to read before you change anything,' said Rick Warren in his hearty endorsement. (Berit Kjos, Part 9, *Dealing with Resisters,* NewsWithViews.com April 9, 2004, p. 46.)

And what do we find? Ominous determination to implement change with the expectation that church leaders will remain informed and apply it or be excised from the body. Everybody, finally, has to agree, for those who won't and who choose to resist,

> are viewed as intolerable barriers to the ultimate goal: a new way of collective thinking, being and serving...What counts is the unity and conformity derived from the common focus, the feel-good group experiences, the peer pressure, and the facilitated process. The only real obstacles to mass compliance are those who oppose the essential steps to top-down control and infect others with their doubts. (Ibid., p. 47.)

Rick Warren is more subtle, and his references to health versus disease cloak his hostility toward "unhealthy" members who resist his agenda. In *The Purpose Driven Church*, he writes: "When a human body is out of balance we call that disease....Likewise, when the body of Christ becomes unbalanced, disease occurs....Health will occur only when everything is brought back into balance. The task of church leadership is to discover and remove growth-restricting diseases and barriers so that natural, normal growth can occur." (Ibid., Rick Warren, *The Purpose Driven Church*, p. 16.)

In a similar way the New Age movement is pointing out biblical Christians and others as well who eventually cannot unite with the religious unity of the universal spiritual New Age hierarchy. They are considered to be a menace to the well-being of humanity and compared with a cancerous tumor that needs to be cut out.

> It is like watching a cancer grow; something must be done before the whole body is destroyed... (*The Omega letter*, Oct. 1988, vol. 3, no. 9, p. 12.)

> ...when a form proves inadequate, or too diseased, or too crippled...it is...no disaster when that form has to go. Death is not a disaster to be feared; the work of the destroyer is not really cruel or undesirable...Therefore, there is much destruction permitted by the Custodians of the Plan and much evil turned into good... (Alice Bailey, *Education in the New Age*, pp. 111, 112.)

> Removing a person's cancer, no matter how painful, is doing him a favor and the New Agers also believe that removing those who disagree with them is doing a favor to both the individual and the group as a whole. (Dr. Cathy Burns, *Billy Graham and his Friends,* Second Printing, 2002, Sharing, Mt. Carmel, PA, p. 545.)

A short impression of the recommended steps towards those that do not collaborate to make the hidden plan succeed, is as follows:

1. Identify resisters. In the church-growth movement the opponents are especially those who question the need for systematic change; who distrust the dialectic process and reject the transformational programs and methods.

2. Assess resisters and determine the degree of resistance.

3. Make friends with borderline opponents; enlist them as much as possible and convince them that they should agree. Some will reconsider their objections and adapt to the demands of the group. Others will withdraw in silence. Rick Warren writes:

   > For unity's sake, we must never let differences divide us. We must stay focused on what matters most—learning to love each other as Christ has loved us, and fulfilling God's five purposes for each of us and his church. (*The Purpose Driven Church*, pp. 161, 162.)

This sounds good and plausible, but Berit Kjos rightly asks the question:

> But how can concerned Christians embrace a unity that involves compromising the truth? Only if our primary focus is fixed on Jesus and His Word can we truly share His agape love in a darkening world. For His name's sake, we can't let a human vision of unity force us to minimize His truth. (Berit Kjos, Part 9, *Dealing with Resisters*, 2004, p. 49.)

There is little tolerance for a positive Biblical position without any compromise, for this stands in the way of their aims and programs for total and continual change. The advice is that the leaders should promote the vision as broadly as possible and "steadily break down the residual places of resistance." (Ibid., p. 49.)

4. The more persistent resisters must be marginalized. They delay progress and undermine the needed unity, momentum and passion for change.

That's why pastors often suggest to "divisive" members that they might be happier elsewhere...Some loss of members is likely throughout the change process...The worst mistake is to compromise the vision to try to retain a few members. (Ibid., p. 50.)

Indeed, such a forced unity can only be effective by subjecting and silencing unsupportive members and waiving all discussion of subjects upon which not all do agree.

Says Ellen White:

> The wide diversity of belief in the Protestant churches is regarded by many as decisive proof that no effort to secure a forced uniformity can ever be made. But there has been for years, in churches of the Protestant faith, a strong and growing sentiment in favor of a union based upon common points of doctrine. To secure such a union, the discussion of subjects upon which all were not agreed— however important they might be from a Bible standpoint—must necessarily be waived. (*The Great Controversy,* p. 444.)

This in fact is what we see forcefully applied in a very unbiblical way.

The leaders must be prepared to deal with members who refuse to leave the church and choose to stay by their point of view. This cannot be tolerated. "...failure to act on the problem is far worse than the cure. The Bible gives clear principles in Matthew 18 for how to handle these conflicts." (Ibid.)

Yes, indeed, the Bible does give clear principles. But Matthew 18, shows us how to deal with sinners who have transgressed God's law. This Bible passage does not tell us how to handle those who follow the voice of their conscience in faithful obedience to God's Word and are not prepared to make any compromise and who, accordingly, take their stand.

Yet, in spite of the enforced tolerance toward moral and spiritual sins within the Church Growth Movement, there is little tolerance toward those who appear to disobey the top-down mandates of this manipulative management system. Sold out to pragmatism, it often turns a blind eye to Scriptures such as Acts 5:29, 'We must obey God rather than man.' (Ibid.)

5. Vilify those who choose to stay and fight.

At this stage, negative labels, accusations and slander are permitted, if not encouraged, to circulate. Resisters—now labeled as divisive trouble-makers—are blamed for disunity, for slowing the change process, and for distracting the church body from wholehearted focus on its all-important vision, mission or purpose. Ponder the subtle suggestions and negative labels Pastor Warren attaches to individuals who question his purpose-driven management system:

'The Bible knows nothing of solitary saints or spiritual hermits isolated from other believers and deprived of fellowship...Today's culture of independent individualism has created many spiritual orphans—'bunny believers' who hop around from one church to another without any identity, accountability or commitments...Many believe one can be a 'good Christian' without joining (or even attending) a local church, but God would strongly disagree...A church family moves you out of self-centered isolation...Isolation breeds deceitfulness.' (Ibid., pp. 50, 51. Rick Warren, *The Purpose Driven Life,* 2002, pp. 130, 133, 134; as quoted by Berit Kjos.)

Why does Warren specify this so particularly?

Commenting on Warren's statements, Berit Kjos continues:

> Notice the derogatory implication in each statement. We discussed some of God's special 'solitary saints' earlier. Trusting God alone, they grew strong in Spirit. Those who have searched long and hard for a Biblical church with solid teaching and edifying fellowship may identify with what Rick Warren mocks as 'bunny believers.' And the 'isolation' of a faithful Christian who obeys God's call to separation from worldliness and unbiblical fellowship produces purity, not deceitfulness (2 Cor. 6:12—18). (Ibid. p. 51.)
>
> Yet unfair and misleading labels continue to undermine the credibility of faithful believers. In a review of the book, *'Making Change Happen One Person at a Time: Assessing Change Capacity Within Your Organization,'* resisters were labeled 'tares in a wheat field.' In other words, a negative Biblical image was used to disgrace those who couldn't conform. Those who flowed with the change were the 'wheat field.' Resisters were tares...No doubt many are being deceived. And all who embrace this process of 'managed change' tend to share its hostility toward resisters. (Ibid.)

Berit Kjos gives the example of an Australian minister who was disciplined by the head minister and the elders because he dared to address the errors of the way that was followed and to challenge the vision and church programs that were hurting more people than healing them. This pastor testifies: "my wife and I soon found ourselves 'churchless.'" (Ibid.)

6. Make rules, regulations, laws and principles that will put opponents to silence, rebuke and punish them and drive them out. In the Saddleback church of Rick Warren each new member has to sign a *Membership Covenant*. "It includes this innocuous promise: 'I will protect the unity of my church...by following the leaders.'" (Ibid., p. 52.)

This declaration is supported by Scripture-passages such as: "Let no corrupt communication proceed out of your mouth," (Eph. 4:29) and "Obey them that have the rule over you, and submit yourselves." (Hebrews 13:17.)

But to openly choose to follow the rules of the Bible and to testify thereof, can never be regarded as corrupt communication.

Berit Kjos explains:

> And, if church leaders followed the world's management system rather than God's way, the command to 'obey your leader and submit....' would be overruled by other relevant Scriptures. For example, when the religious leaders in Jerusalem told John and Peter to stop teaching 'in the name of Jesus,' they answered, 'Whether it is right in the sight of God to listen to you more than to God, you judge. For we cannot but speak the things which we have seen and heard.' Acts 4:19. (Ibid., p. 52.)

E. G. White warns:

> Satan is constantly endeavoring to attract attention to man in the place of God. He leads the people to look to bishops, to pastors, to professors of theology, as their guides...Then, by controlling the minds of these leaders, he can influence the multitudes according to his will...Fearful is the issue to which the world is to be brought. The powers of earth, uniting to war...will decree that all...shall conform to the customs of the church by the observance of the false sabbath. All who refuse compliance will be visited with civil penalties, and it will finally be declared that they are deserving of death. (*Great Controversy*, pp. 595, 604.)

Dr. Burns informs us.

A former New Ager, Randall Baer, states that those who refuse the mark of the beast will be targeted for extermination in what would euphemistically be called re-education centers of love and relocation, that is, death camps in disguise. (Burns, *Billy Graham and his Friends*, Sharing, Mt. Carmel, PA, Second Printing, 2002, p. 545.)

Rick Warren expects agreement without any criticism, in order to receive God's blessing.

> God blesses churches that are unified. At Saddleback Church, every member signs a covenant that includes a promise to protect the unity of our fellowship. As a result, the church has never had a conflict that split the fellowship. (*The Purpose Driven Life*, p. 167.)

Third, never criticize what God is blessing, even though it may be a style of ministry that makes you feel uncomfortable. (*The Purpose Driven Church*, p. 62.)

He who cannot listen to the leaders, for reasons of principle, is in fact always wrong; he causes pain and trouble and makes things hard and God will hold him responsible.

Listen to their counsel…Contribute to the joy of their leadership, not its drudgery. Why would you want to make things harder for them?…You will give an account to God of how well you followed your leaders. (*The Purpose Driven Life*, p. 166.)

Initially, as to those who find it difficult to follow his program, Warren's words were still somewhat covered and mild, however, as time went on his tone became more and more clear as well as severe.

Now, if these resisters, who are often sincere and dear people, could even be regarded as tares, the Bible clearly teaches us that **they should not be gathered up** since also the wheat may be rooted up with them. Both should grow together until the harvest. (Matt. 13:29, 30.)

But the policy of Saddleback is to get rid of those opposing the new program. They are standing in the way of Purpose Driven progress.

Rick Warren openly declared on his website in a June 14th article with regard to churches that have been plateaued for several months or years: "I'm saying some people **are going to have to die or leave."** (Emphasis added.)

This sounds similar to the words written by a well known New Ager, Barbara Marx Hubbard. Those not prepared to follow the New Age program are going to die:

When the word of this hope has reached the nations, the end of this phase of evolution shall come. All will know their choice. All will be required to choose…All who choose not to evolve **will die off**. (Barbara Marx Hubbard, *Happy Birthday Planet Earth*, Ocean Tree Books, Hemet, CA 92344, 1986, p. 17. Emphasis added.)

That indeed Purpose Driven Resisters are forced to leave may be well illustrated by a report:

> The phone calls and emails started coming in about three years ago. Sometimes the caller was in his mid-eighties, sometimes the caller was crying. But all of them had the same kind of story to tell—when their churches decided to get involved with 40 Days of Purpose, everything began changing and when they questioned these changes, they each soon found themselves silenced, ostracized and eventually without a church to attend. Now today, nearly five years after *Purpose Driven Life* was released, thousands of believers are scattered throughout the world, having been ridiculed and demoralized for even just the slightest questioning of the Purpose Driven program. In one email we received, the young man was handed a letter from his pastor. The letter had been written by a Saddleback field representative who told the pastor to do what he had to do to get rid of those opposing the new program. (*Lighthouse Newsletter,* June 23, 2006. Cf., *Truth Set Free,* A Christian Discernment Community, *Purpose Driven Resisters—Leave or Die.*)

The internationally well known *Wall Street Journal* clearly indicates that the Purpose Driven movement should not be considered lightly. Several instances of disastrous results and seriously divided churches are listed while we read: **"But the purpose-driven movement is dividing the country's more than 50 million evangelicals."** (Suzanne Sataline, *Veneration Gap, A Popular Strategy For Church Growth Splits Congregants Across U.S., Members Divide On Making Sermons, Music More 'Purpose-Driven' No More 'Wrath of God'?,* September 5, 2006; Page A1.)

Leonard Sweet, Warren's co-worker, explains that it is time for a "Postmodern Reformation" and everybody must choose: "Reinvent yourself for the 21st century **or die."** (Leonard Sweet, *Soul Tsunami,* Zondervan, 1999, p. 75. Emphasis added.)

Rick Warren's Purpose Driven program is supported by Dan Southerland, director of Church Transitions Inc., a training organization for Pastors and church leaders to accomplish transitions within the church. Warren endorsed Southerland's book *Transitioning* and recommends it on his Pastor's website. Annually Southerland teaches this transition process at Saddleback's Purpose Driven Conference.

Note how Southerland compares those who criticize the program with Sanballat who resisted Nehemia's work. (Neh. 4.) He characterizes them as **leaders from hell**. If you have someone who opposes the Purpose Driven plans, Southerland cautions to be diplomatic:

You cannot call this guy a leader from hell to his face - but you could call him Sanballat." (*Transitioning: Leading Your Church Through Change*, Zondervan, 2000, 2002, p. 115.)

Is it a Christ-like attitude to denote church members as Sanballats and leaders from hell because they find it difficult to follow the modern transitioning program?

Is it, in order to attain unity, in accordance with the Bible when church leaders force believing Christians, who cannot agree with their plans, to leave the church?

Can such a unity enforced by the leaders bear God's approval and be blessed by Him? Will blessing, unity and church-growth come through the strict following of modern strategies of behaviour adaption, as is also applied on the economical and social plane? Or can we expect blessing, unity and church-growth through the working of the Holy Spirit, when we are sanctified in the truth of His Word and united in Christ? (John 17:17–23; Zech. 4:6).

Pastors and church members have similar obligations to stand for the truth. A true revival must take place. Mac Dominick writes:

> Apathy is a huge issue in Bible-believing churches. However, the time has come for the 'pew-dwellers' to 'grow a backbone' and stand for biblical principles. So many members will not do anything that 'rocks the boat,' but the issues demand that lay people 'stand in the gap' and defend the Word of God…**Church members have an obligation to hold their pastor accountable to the Word of God. Those who do this in the face of new paradigm transitioning attempts will, without question, be accused of 'not supporting the pastor.' But men and women who are willing to be 'Defenders of the Faith' must stand firm on the truth in the face of these accusations.** (Mac Dominick, *Outcome-Based Religion: Purpose, Apostasy, & The New Paradigm Church,* 2005, p. 330. Emphasis added.)

Chapter 33

Critical Voices

Many Christians are not happy with the modern developments within the church. These feel that the church is not in accordance with God's intention.

L. P. Meyers protests ominously:

> Today, church has become a field of marketing and politics. The goal of filling buildings, still seems to be of primary importance... When will we wake up, and start being the church that God called us to be? When will we leave behind the selfish ways of man, and begin to partake of the true and undefiled religion that God had intended?...There is no hope for the church, if we continue in the paths we are walking. There is no hope of seeing Christ manifest in the believers, if we continue this course. We will not see the manifestation of the sons of God, if we do not leave behind this evil spirit, forsake tradition, and turn to the true and living God, with hearts of repentance. There will be no promised land for the church as it is today. (*This Church is not appearing Glorious and it does not seem to be Purpose Driven*, Pleasant Word, 2004, pp. 120, 121.)

John F. MacArthur describes the modern "User-Friendly Church" and writes:

> Scripture says the early Christians 'turned the world upside down' (Acts 17:6, KJV). In our generation the world is turning the church upside down. Biblically, God is sovereign, not 'unchurched Harry.' The Bible, not a marketing plan, is supposed to be the sole blueprint and final authority for all church ministry. Ministry should meet peoples' real needs, not salve their selfishness. And the Lord of the church is Christ, not some couch potato with the remote control in his hand. (*Ashamed of the Gospel, When The Church Becomes*

Like The World, Crossway Books, 1993, p. 51.)

Os Guinness discusses the unbiblical points and shortcomings of the mega churches and he gives us several warnings as well as seven main tips for discernment as to the dangers of the church-growth movement. Although there may be a great harvest it may also lead to a form of Christianity "that makes a mockery of the gospel and of the seriousness of the hour." He also writes:

> First, many megachurches make much of their front-door statistics (who comes and why) but less of their back-door statistics that are even more revealing (who leaves and why). Then, suddenly, like fast-growing insurance companies whose unrenewed policies exceed their new policies, they decline or collapse. Second, a very large part of church-growth success in the West (as much as 80 percent in America, some say) is growth by **transfer, not conversion**. As Jim Petersen of the Navigators says: "Increase of this sort isn't church growth at all. It's just a reshuffling of the same fifty-two cards." (*Dining with the Devil, The Megachurch Movement Flirts with Modernity,* Baker Book House, 1993, pp. 81, 82. Emphasis added.)

James Sundquist writes about Warren's popular book, everywhere so diligently studied in a *40-day spiritual journey*:

> After reading '*The Purpose Driven Life,*' I could not help but wonder how it ever made it past the editors at Zondervan, his publisher, because there were so many colossal biblical blunders in the book. (*Who's Driving the Purpose Driven Church?* Rock Salt Publ., 2004, p. 15.)

As to Warren's use of the Bible, Sundquist writes: "Using terms not even in the original text is a persistent pattern of Rick Warren adding to, subtracting from, omitting critical qualifiers, and changing words and concepts in the Bible." (Ibid., p. 39.)

And Warren Smith, formerly involved in the New Age movement, writes, after exposing several New Age teachings in Warren's book:

> Sadly, if Rick Warren and other Christian leaders fall for New Age schemes and devices rather than exposing them, they will take countless numbers of sincere people down with them. It will be the blind leading the blind, as they fall further and fur-

ther into the deceptive ditch of the New Age and its New Spirituality. Undiscerning Christians, who think they are on 'the narrow way' preparing the way for Jesus Christ, may discover too late that they had actually been on 'the broad way' preparing for the Antichrist. It is not too late to warn everyone, but it must be done soon before the deception advances any further. As we have already seen, there is 'another Jesus,' 'another Christ,' 'another spirit' and 'another gospel' at work in the world. The Church must not continue to fall prey to the deception. And the Church must not give in to the teachings of a 'New Spirituality' that promises world peace but may ultimately cost you your soul...

In these times of heightened danger and treacherous deception, we must always go to the Lord for truth and direction. Christians following deceived leaders will only end up deceived themselves. We must always measure everything by the true Word of God...May we always have a love of the truth. May God give us wisdom and spiritual discernment as we seek to contend for the faith. And may God give us all the strength and courage and conviction to endure the challenging times that are before us. (*Deceived On Purpose, The New Age Implications of the Purpose-Driven Church,* Second Edition, Mountain Stream Press, 2005, pp. 179, 180.)

Richard W. O'Ffill, retired Pastor, Revivalist and Adult Ministries Director, Florida Conference, writes:

We are not wrong in trying to be more effective in retaining our children and grandchildren in the church. We cannot be faulted for wanting to revive the church in places where it has seemingly stagnated, but in going to the Willow Creek and Saddleback churches of the world we have been fooled...

O'Ffill continues,

Our brethren in the churches who have in recent years become aficionados of Willow Creek and others like it may have been well-intentioned, but experience has proved that the experiment has been divisive to our church; and the casualties to churches, their pastors, and members has been significant...Friend, in spite of our best intentions, we have been, as it were, 'Trojan-horsed'! The evidence is in, and we have been fooled. What we had hoped for is not what we have gotten. Let's ask the Lord to forgive us for unbelief...For lack of faith we have allowed ourselves to believe cunningly devised fables. Our brothers and sisters in other denominations need the message of our church more than we need their methods. God's last message for His people just before He returns to take them home will not be finished by the might and power of marketing methods, nor by the megachurches that are the Willow Creeks or Saddlebacks, 'but by My Spirit, saith the Lord' (Zechariah 4:6). (*Here We Stand, Evaluating New Trends in the Church*, Review and Herald Graphics, Hagerstown, MD, 2005, p. 21.)

E. Bruce Price, retired Pastor, Evangelist, and Departmental Director, South Pacific Division, testifies:

> When I did not make my church a celebration-type contemporary church, some church administrators questioned why I was not being 'progressive.' I told them that when this celebration movement should be successful and prove that this was the way the Lord wanted His church to go, then I would follow. Until then I would wait. But as I waited and watched, I witnessed only disasters in both Australia and the U.S.A... To bring souls to a full and saving knowledge of Jesus Christ takes much dedication, prayer, and work. Nothing has changed in this regard since the days of Jesus, His disciples, or Paul. There are no shortcuts. We are to solidly build on the Rock, not superficially on the sand! (Ibid., pp. 26, 33.)

It is very clear that not everybody feels comfortable with the popular changes that take place in so many churches. Several church leaders do discern the dangers of the church-growth positions and teaching. Particularly the new contemplative spirituality with its various meditative practices causes much concern.

For instance Calvary Distribution, a resource ministry of the Calvary Chapel movement founded by Pastor Chuck Smith, discontinued Rick Warren's products, such as *The Purpose Driven Life,* declaring,

> The teaching and positions of Rick Warren have come into conflict with us as Calvary Chapel. (*Recall Notice—Discontinued Items,* June, 2006, Calvary Chapel Distribution website.)

Roger Oakland, for many years affiliated with Calvary Chapel, stresses some fundamental reasons for removing all Purpose Driven materials from distribution. He points out differences in Eschatology—differences with regard to the Emerging Church—differences with regard to contemplative prayer and mysticism—differences with regard to church growth principles and beliefs.

He explains that Pastor Chuck Smith

> has expressed serious concerns about the Purpose Driven church growth movement. On numerous occasions he made the point that the Calvary way, was not the Purpose Driven way. He made it clear that healthy church growth should be centered on the teaching of the Word of God and not on methods derived by human effort. From the beginning of the Calvary Chapel movement, Chuck has emphasized being 'spirit led' rather than being motivated by a humanistic agenda put in place by church growth experts. (Roger Oakland, *Understand the Times International, Calvary Chapel and Purpose Driven,* July 17, 2006.)

Oakland emphasizes that Warren has a different eschatological outlook.

> Warren encourages his followers to ignore Bible prophecy and spend their time and energy on the here and now, in order to establish a man made social plan (P.E.A.C.E. Plan) that will make planet earth a better place for everyone... Rick Warren's Purpose Driven P.E.A.C.E. Plan is part of a plan that is intended to establish the Kingdom of God here on earth before Jesus returns. This Kingdom depends on human effort. He is willing to work with governments... political leaders...the United Nations...and even the Roman Catholic Church. [...] In April of 2005, Rick Warren, speaking to 25,000 in attendance at Anaheim Stadium, encouraged his Purpose Driven supporters to partner with him to usher in the Kingdom of God on planet earth, right now... It is important to understand that this type of teaching that Rick Warren heavily promotes is very similar to New Age teachings that say the endtimes, according to the book of Revelation, does not have to happen if enough people come together, realize their unity with each other and with God, and strive towards global peace. (Ibid.)

Oakland concludes,

> It would seem to me that 'Purpose Driven' mixed together with a touch of mysticism could be considered a recipe for spiritual disaster. That is especially true in these days when so many Christians are willing to embrace eastern mystical practices like 'yoga' and other methods to pursue a state of silence or quietness in order to get into an altered state of consciousness. This is not the message

> that Pastor Chuck Smith or Calvary Distribution would want to promote…In my view, the stand Pastor Chuck Smith made to stay with the Word of God and warn the flock about the imminent return of Jesus was biblical and the correct decision. I personally believe that those who go down the road of Purpose Driven will be come less and less discerning regarding the end times scenario that is currently unfolding, which clearly reveals that Jesus may be soon returning. I also believe that it won't be very long before Rick Warren and his Purpose Driven theology will join hands with Roman Catholicism so that together they may work toward their common goal of ushering in the 'Kingdom of God.' (Ibid.)

There are some 700 affiliated Chapels. Calvary Chapel of Costa Mesa has as many as 30,000 people in its congregation each week. (Gwen Newton, *The Religious Movements Page: Calvary Chapel*, 1998, update 29-11-2001.)

This attitude of Calvary Chapel is recommendable. We should always be alert since New Age concepts and unbiblical meditation practices are subtly introduced into many churches.

Note also the firm stand the Bible Presbyterian denomination took:

> At its 69th General Synod, the Bible Presbyterian denomination urged congregations and 'all believers of whatever denomination' to **fiercely repudiate and expose** the 'egregious error' espoused by Rick Warren and other proponents of the 'purpose-driven paradigm' (PDP) of church growth, reported John T. Dyck, Assistant Clerk of Synod. The denomination cited several problems with the PDP:
>
> 1. The entire strategy is based upon the concept that unbelievers are seeking after God, in spite of the fact that the Bible could not be clearer to the contrary;
>
> 2. The PDP values the opinions of unbelievers more than the opinions of God as revealed in His Word, believing that 'felt needs' should dictate what is said from the pulpit;
>
> 3. The PDP asserts that Christians must think like non-Christians to reach them;
>
> 4. The PDP believes God is not concerned with the manner of

His creatures' entering into His presence;

5. The PDP misunderstands the nature of the church, ignoring the Biblical teaching that the institution and worship of the church exists for the glorification of God Himself and the edification of believers. (*Baptist Bulletin, Main News September 05,* Submitted by Norm Olson on Thu, 2005-09-01. Emphasis added.)

A part of the "Bible Presbyterian Church Resolution 69:13" says:

The essential problem with the PDP is that man is unabashedly the measure of all things (Judges 21:25). This problem results in numerous erroneous approaches to the ministry of the Church...We call upon Mr. Warren to repent of his heretical teachings. **We are resolved to stand firm against this perversion of Biblical Christianity, and guard against its insidious intrusion into the lives of our churches.** (Adopted by the 69th General Synod of the Bible Presbyterian Church, meeting in Olympia, WA, OH, August 4–9, 2005. Emphasis added.)

Shouldn't we follow this courageous example and make a similar resolution?

Chapter 34

Angels

When the cosmic Christ comes, he will send angels to teach, instruct and help the people.

> It might be of interest here to point out that when He comes Whom angels and men await, and Whose work it is to inaugurate the new age...He will bring with Him some of the great Angels...for the helping of the race...When what they have to impart is apprehended by the race, physical ills and sickness will be offset...These...angels are a band of servers, pledged to the service of the Christ, and their work is to contact men and to teach them along certain lines. (Alice Bailey, *The Externalisation of the Hierarchy*, Lucis Press, p. 508.)

"The cosmic Christ," indeed. This has not reference to the Christ of the Bible, but to a New Age Christ whom they claim to be neither human nor divine. It is none other than the Satanic anti-Christ. And angels? He has a third of heaven's angels who fell with him at his command.

Will Baron, a former New Age priest, described a visit to the Kenneth Copeland Convention in Anaheim. Copeland told how God had given him a vision.

> I heard him describe how he had recently been given a vision from God. I heard Copeland say that God had told him that Jesus would soon begin to appear in a physical form in the churches. Jesus, perhaps accompanied by his angels, would be seen walking down the aisles and then would disappear. This would occur in several churches with increasing frequency. The statement I heard was like dynamite in my ears. Wow, I thought, this is interesting. Muriel had predicted exactly the same thing. She had recently told us at the Lighted Way that we could expect Jesus to appear during our church

service. (*Deceived by the New Age,* Pacific Press, 1990, p. 108.)

Notice what E. G. White has written:

> A power from beneath is working to bring about the last great scenes in the drama—Satan coming as Christ...Satan will use every opportunity to seduce men from their allegiance to God. He and the angels who fell with him will appear on the earth as men, seeking to deceive. God's angels also will appear as men, and will use every means in their power to defeat the purposes of the enemy...Evil angels in the form of men will talk with those who know the truth. They will misinterpret and misconstrue the statements of the messengers of God... (*Last Day Events,* p. 160, 162.)

This is an ominous statement in light of the many within the church who consistently "misinterpret and misconstrue the statements of" God's own messenger for this day. Does it not suggest that they are already so being led?

Note the implications of the following warning in light of the challenge from the Church Growth specialists and New Age proponents. Fortunately, divine warnings are accompanied by hope.

> We are engaged in a warfare against the hosts of darkness. Unless we follow our Leader closely, Satan will obtain the victory over us...Evil angels in the form of believers will work in our ranks to bring in a strong spirit of unbelief. Let not even this discourage you, but bring a true heart to the help of the Lord against the powers of satanic agencies. These powers of evil will assemble in our meetings, not to receive a blessing, but to counterwork the influences of the Spirit of God...It is not difficult for the evil angels to represent both saints and sinners who have died, and make these representations visible to human eyes. These manifestations will be more frequent, and developments of a more startling character will appear as we near the close of time...The enemy is preparing to deceive the whole world by his miracle-working power. He will assume to personate the angels of light, to personate Jesus Christ...The sick will be healed before us. Miracles will be performed in our sight. Are we prepared for the trial which awaits us when the lying wonders of Satan shall be more fully exhibited? (*Last Day Events*, pp. 160, 161, 162, 166.)

Satan and his angels work powerfully to deceive the whole world by mighty signs and lying wonders. Will the saints be misled? Will they also worship Satan? Angels of God are about them! And although they may be threatened with death, they can be assured that God will protect them.

> Could men see with heavenly vision, they would behold companies of angels that excel in strength stationed about those who have kept the word of Christ's patience. With sympathizing tenderness, angels have witnessed their distress and have heard their prayers…their enemies…will endeavor to take their lives. But none can pass the mighty guardians stationed about every faithful soul. Some are assailed in their flight from the cities and villages; but the swords raised against them break and fall powerless as a straw. Others are defended by angels in the form of men of war. (*The Great Controversy*, pp. 630, 631.)

Chapter 35

Drums

Matthew Fox, a prominent occultist and new ager, informs us that the coming cosmic Christ demands a complete change of worship. Note that the Eucharist and the influence of the dance on the beat of the drum are especially stressed in the following quotes:

> The coming of the Cosmic Christ will mean a thorough renewal of worship in the West...Worship is the playing out of the cosmic drama in our psyches and social groupings...Living worship, based on a living cosmology, creates a people and heals a people; it celebrates a people and their amazing place in the universe...as a performance of the cosmic drama in our soul and in the social gathering. Living worship, based on a living cosmology creates and heals man; it celebrates a people with an amazing place in the universe. (Fox, *The Coming of the Cosmic Christ,* Harper & Row, 1988, pp. 211, 212.)

The intense focus on "cosmic" and "cosmology," metaphysical terms referring to the universe, which is itself regarded as god and thus considered to be alive, is a New Age earmark. Thus, Fox speaks of "living worship, based on a living cosmology."

He continues, with blasphemous reference to the "cosmic Christ," who is declared neither human nor divine:

> The eucharist stands as a complete affirmation of the Cosmic Christ's yearning for intimacy with the human ones—that is, the Cosmic Christ's need to be eaten. All of creation is present at such a moment, such a feast and festal gathering—no one is excluded for this is truly a cosmological event. (Ibid., pp. 214, 215.)

Consider the role of the dance and the drum in worship, and remember that "cosmic Christ" does not refer to Jesus, but to Satan himself, the great anti-Christ who will mimic Christ's return. Note the impersonal "its" in reference to "the cosmic Christ":

> The Cosmic Christ wants to dance, to express itself bodily, to respond to Good News and to cosmic grace. (Ibid., p. 217.)

> Not books, but body and heart prayer will reawaken us to living ritual. (Ibid., p. 219.)

Thus the use of Bible or song book is discouraged.

Again, lessons abound from the native peoples of the power of dancing together with the beating of the drum providing a common heartbeat. This heartbeat reminds us of the time in our mother's womb when we were so much at peace; it reminds us of the heartbeat of Mother Earth—beating still on our behalf; it reminds us of the heartbeat of the Cosmic Christ which fills the universe with overflowing, wet love binding all things together on earth and in heaven. (Ibid., p. 218.)

> It is time to place worship within the cosmological setting that the human species throughout the world is embracing. We should explore the rituals of the native peoples, whose ceremonies appreciated the power of darkness and night. Sweat lodges, for example, allow us to be immersed in the holy darkness of our origins in the womb. The great ceremonial dances are another example: They often take place during the night when the drum is best heard in heart as well as in head and body, and when fire takes on special meaning. Moon rituals may threaten a light-oriented patriarchal slant on worship, but for that very reason they ought to be explored for their power to evoke mystery and to call forth the spirit as embodied in women's experience through the centuries. (Ibid., p. 221.)

This is a direct call for return to Pagan worship.

> Worship will be the gathering place where the many stories are told and retold by dance, poetry, music, color, song, laughter, drama, and art forms still to be created. Renewed worship will allure the youth to dream bigger dreams, to test their incipient adulthood with visions of greatness...Protestants, Catholics, and Jews alike are today yearning for the vitality and rebirth that a living worship can

bring about." (Ibid., pp. 224, 225.)

As we have noticed, the modern church-growth movement is clearly infected with occult new Age thinking. Is it then any wonder that we see these things Fox describes taking place more and more in many churches today? There is dance, song, laughter, drama and modern art forms that replace the conservative forms of worship. Should we be astonished as we see the introduction of popular music and drum bands in so many churches?

The introduction of Christian rock music into the church is not accidental but plays a purpose driven role in the hidden agenda. The churches need to experience the "paradigm shift"—the radical transition—and the rock beat of the popular Christian music is a perfect instrument of a manipulating sort.

David Tame writes,

> ...music is more than a language. It is the language of languages. It can be said that of all the arts, there is none other that more powerfully moves and changes the consciousness...it is rock with which we must deal today...Its effect upon the soul is to make nigh-impossible the true inner silence and peace necessary for the contemplation of eternal verities...How necessary it is in this age for some to have the courage to be the ones who are 'different,' and to separate themselves out from the pack who long ago sold their lives and personalities to this sound and the anti-Aquarian culture which has sprung up around it!...The notion that music has no effect upon man, or that all music is harmless, is absolutely in error. (David Tame, *The Secret Power of Music*, Destiny Books, 1984, pp. 151, 204, 141.)

Investigation has shown that music affects digestion, internal secretions, circulation, nutrition and respiration. Even the neural networks of the brain have been found to be sensitive to harmonic principles...If the musician is playing his instrument, then he and his instrument can also be said to be 'playing' the bodies and minds of the audience...Research has discovered rock music to be bad for digestion; it is also dangerous while driving. Further, since rock raises the blood pressure, it is bad for cases of pre-existing hypertension. And since the heartbeat in turn affects one's mood and emotions, these too become subject to the influence of rock rhythms when they are heard, tension and in harmony of the mind being increased. Indeed, rhythm affects not only our bodies, minds and emotions, but even our subconscious. (Ibid., pp. 136-138.)

> Music influences virtually every physical, intellectual and emotional process...Music can even change chromosomes. (Ibid., backcover.)

Some modern effects of music, such as "musicogenic epilepsy," may even stimulate suicide. David Tame explains:

> Some of its victims have been tormented to the point of committing suicide or of murder. Seventy-six cases of this malady have been documented, but there are no doubt many other sufferers who simply do not realize the source of their problem and have received no specific treatment. In each documented case the sufferer experienced seizures which were brought on by certain kinds of music, though the causative music was different in different cases. (Ibid., p. 140.)

Although not realized nor admitted by many, the influence of Christian rock music is definitely not harmless. Its debasing influence is sure and must never be underestimated.

The influence of rock is without doubt comprehensive, which is scientifically undeniably established. It is for instance also very striking that when the 16 year old Jeff Weise killed 10 victims, including himself, on March 21, 2005 in Minnesota, rock music seemed to have played an important role. A fellow student, Sondra Hegstrom, declared that Jeff listened to hard popular music and often spoke about death. (MSNBC 23/3/2005.)

The present church-growth movement with the Alpha course, Willow Creek, Saddleback, and many other churches, are following exactly the occult New Age plan. The emphasis is laid on a "contemporary packing of modern music, singing, drama, multimedia, and practical themes. And...it works!" (*Folder Pijler Conferentie Lelystad*, 2003, Willow Creek Nederland.)

Rick Warren declared at the Super Conference (at Jerry Falwell's Liberty University) in 2003, where about 13,000 ministers and students were present:

> I believe that one of the major church issues [of the future] will be how we're going to reach the next generation with our music... You can make more people mad with music than anything else in church.... I'll be honest with you, we are loud. We are really, really loud on a weekend service.... I say, 'We're not gonna turn it down.' Now the reason why is baby boomers want to feel the music, not just hear it.... God loves variety. (Dennis Costella, *Foundation Magazine*, March-April, 1998. Cf., Rick Warren, *Selecting Worship Music*, July 29, 2002.)

Drums are found in many churches and the services nowadays have more in common with rock-concerts than with a sacred church service. Musical bands, pop singers, and also New Agers (Gannin and John Tesh) are without any problem switched on at Willow Creek and Saddleback. Rick Warren writes that in the beginning at Saddleback everything was presented:

> We used classical, country, jazz, rock, reggae, easy listening, and even rap. The crowd never knew what was coming next. (*The Purpose Driven Church*, p. 280.)

Rick Warren admits:

> Saddleback is unapologetically a contemporary music church. We've often been referred to in the press as '**The flock that likes to rock**.' We use the style of music the majority of people in our church listen to on the radio. (Rick Warren, *Selecting Worship Music*. Emphasis added.)

So you will have noticed, the music that is presented in the church can also be heard in the world. Why then is there such an emphasis laid on such music in the church? What is the special thing about it if it can be heard everywhere in the world? For that kind of music then you don't have a need to go to church, do you?

> ...many believe that the only effective way to reach this new generation is to incorporate rock music and the drum set into the worship service. But I know from experience that such thinking is flawed. I came to know the truth at the time when I was deeply involved in rock and jazz. The blending of this music with worship was unattractive, and almost laughable, because if I really wanted to hear that music I would go to a place where it came from: the world.

> And young people who are honest realize that their experience in church should be different than what they receive from the world. (Karl Tsatalbasidis, *Drums, Rock, and Worship*, p. 65.)

> Every uncouth thing will be demonstrated. There will be shouting, with drums, music, and dancing. The senses of rational beings will become so confused that they cannot be trusted to make right decisions. And this is called the moving of the Holy Spirit. (E. G. White, *Maranatha*, p. 234.)

> 'New Age' linked with 'Christian' would have put up bright red flags a few years ago but not so today…In years gone by this type of music would never have been debated among Bible believing Baptists but today many of them have followed Rick Warren's and Saddleback's methods, message and music philosophy. Why have they gone this direction?…They sought not to the LORD, but rather to other church growth experts, to Saddleback and Willow Creek!!… Is the church of the Risen Lord at liberty to use just any music in its worship? I think not!…The roots of the apostolic and early church were in its preaching and not in its singing!…Paul…said…that he was always 'ready to preach…the gospel'. Preaching is the main emphasis of the churches God has left here till He comes. (D. C. Bennet, *Bonsai Churches, The Root of Music*, Jan. 28, 2005.)

The church-growth specialists seem to give more time to contemporary music than to the proclamation of the true word.

Rick Warren declares:

> From the first day of the new church I'd put more energy and money into a first-class music ministry that matched our target… The style of music you choose to use in your services will be one of the most critical (and controversial) decisions you make in the life of your church. It may also be the most influential factor in determining who your church reaches for Christ and whether or not your church grows. (*The Purpose Driven Church*, p. 279, 280.)

Is it impossible for the church to grow with conservative music because the modern man can't be reached? Did Christ or His apostles go through the land with a music band and did they proclaim once in a while the Gospel message? Good music is useful and has undoubtedly an elevating influence and value, but the proclamation of the Word is the way to spread the Gospel and to bring people to repentance.

> We are to reach modern man with the Gospel! We are trying to reach GOD with our worship!...The focus of acceptable worship is not the unbeliever but the Lord God Himself...The purpose of Christian music/hymns is to give praise and glory to God. Christian music must be God centered and not man centered...Rock music cannot be sanctified for the Lord's use...Rock music fits a wicked lifestyle. Rock music perfectly fits the bar, the dance hall, the night club, the pool hall, the house of prostitution. Rock music fits the tavern but it does not fit the Lord's house...God calls His people out of the end-time apostasy. The church which gravitates toward ecumenical charismatic music will be moved away from a strong Bible stand. There is a spiritual power behind the Contemporary Christian Music. We, therefore, reject the charismatic movement AND ITS MUSIC...We believe worldly music produces worldliness, sensual music produces sensuality. Most Contemporary Christian Music does not produce holiness of life and separation from the world. (*Fair Dinkum, Free Australian Magazine*, Issue 59, But who is the music for; Charismatic Music. Cf., David W. Cloud, *Fundamental Baptist Information Service*, Oak Harbor, WA 98277.)

Many modern revival songs are objectionable to the sincere Christian. There are often inconspicuous thoughts and ideas woven into it that are occult. The known Christian song:

> '*The River Is Here*'...is New Age to the core. It is void of truth, treats God in a generic fashion, and suggests that God's grace and glory flows from a river. Notice the term, 'And all who touch it can be revived.' Standing in the Brownsville church, I watched almost everyone dance, jump, jerk, shake, or swoon to this song. It captured the crowd, but it absolutely was not the Holy Spirit. (Ibid.)

Chapter 36

Neutral Music?

Rick Warren deals with music as if it was neutral and he wants us to believe that God enjoys all kinds of music:

Worship has nothing to do with the style or volume or speed of a song. God loves all kinds of music because he invented it all—fast and slow, loud and soft, old and new. You probably don't like it all, but God does!...One ethnic group's music can sound like noise to another. But God likes variety and enjoys it all. There is no such thing as 'Christian' music; there are only Christian lyrics. It is the words that make a song sacred, not the tune. There are no spiritual tunes. (*The Purpose Driven Life*, pp. 65, 66.)

But this is truly a huge mistake. Music definitely isn't neutral and it certainly does matter what kind of music is presented and how the musical instruments are played. God absolutely can not enjoy music that is wild or suited for the evocation of spirits and demons.

Don't be deceived and let it be crystal clear: Popular music may attract people but it is not invented by God. It is Satan who likes it but never God.

An interesting story of Giani, a young woman possessed by 37 demons, adequately illustrates this. It happened in Caxias do Sul, Brazil. It took 88 days to liberate this victim. A paragraph taken from the report reads as follows:

> **Many times** during the 88 days before Giani was freed from the last demon, one of them would **taunt and ridicule** one person present or another, saying that they belonged to him. The devil would then mention sins such as novel reading, **listening to popular music,** or wearing makeup, and would say that because the person did

not give these up, they belonged to him. Such encounters caused many of the church members to renew their consecration to God and to give up the sins the devils mentioned. (*Review,* July 4, 1974, p. 20. Emphasis added.)

The report says in a Postscript:

> More than 50 persons have been baptized as a result of Giani's experience. There is not a more consecrated or dedicated church group in this state than the one at Caxias do Sul. (Ibid.)

So it should be clear that real church growth of truly converted people will not be advanced by introducing popular music styles but by *giving up* such music.

It should be given serious thought that the much extolled modern Christian music styles are more likely to attract evil spirits and to dispel heaven's holy angels.

Pastor M. O'Neal, who wrote a book *How Bad Music is Killing Our Fundamental Churches,* writes:

> Rome and the Protestants have gradually been changing their music styles... What I'm talking about is that it has an African beat... Thorough Bible students also know that Africa in general and Egypt in particular are 'types' of the world system. Still, this worldly music is the music that is being played in nearly ALL churches today. The African beat is the driving beat behind rock music, or what is called Contemporary Christian Music, and in slightly modified form is the beat behind country music, or what is called Southern Gospel music. That African, anapestic beat is behind the rock, country, folk, soft rock, and nearly all other forms of contemporary music, whether or not the beat is noticed or recognized by the listener...This music is spiritual music. It involves the spirit world, and it invokes the spirit world. Music is not neutral. It is a powerful entity that may be evil or good in its nature. (M. O'Neal, *How Rome will Recapture the Protestants*, pp. 18-20. P.O. Box 3382, Albany, GA 31706.)

In this context we should remember king Saul's experience. When he was troubled by an evil spirit, his servants gave him the advice to search for someone who could play music for him in order that he may feel better. These servants had enough understanding to realize that music has an influence on the spirit. The king yielded and David was sent for. David wasn't just a good harp player, but it was also known that the Lord was with him. And the Bible tells us: "David took an harp, and played with his hand: so Saul was refreshed, and was well, and the evil spirit departed from him." (1 Sam. 16:23)

If good music can influence the spirit world in our advantage, is it not true then that wrong music will influence the spirits to our disadvantage? Do you doubt that certain music can call up contest, rebellion and prostitution, while other music can cultivate rest, joy, peace and worship?

Jeff Godwin declares:

> Enough evidence now exists to clearly show that when rock is played, our bodies, minds and spirits suffer...Music may be many things but it is NEVER neutral...There is one rule we should never forget. Rock is Rock is Rock is Rock. Whether it's called 'Soft' Rock, 'Acid' Rock, 'Punk' Rock or 'Christian Rock, we are still dealing with music more ancient than the classics. Rooted in the Druid demon worship of Celtic England, and baptized in voodoo ceremonies of Africa and the Caribbean, Satan's rock rules the world...Dozens of scriptures command God's people to separate themselves from the profane. Rock music is an abomination to God, and Christians are supposed to maintain holiness from the world's filth. The C(hristian)-Rock concept erases that line. (Jeff Godwin, *Dancing with Demons*, p. 8, 10, 11, 258.)

It is Jeff Godwin's experience, however, that especially when the unfavourable influence of popular Christian rock music is shown, one usually gets angry, replying with an attitude of how do you dare?— "What gives you the right to judge?" There is often much anger, confusion, denial, delusion and finally a hardened heart and spirit. (*What's wrong with Christian Rock?* Chick Publ., P.O. Box 662, Chino, CA, 1990, chapter 1.)

In rock music as well as in Christian rock there are hidden demonic messages of backward masking and subliminal messages.

Ellen White pointed out: "...every time the church assembles, angels of God are present and evil angels are also present." (Arthur White, *Ellen G. White: The Early Elmshaven Years*, Washington D.C., 1981, p. 74.)

She also stated: "...he (Satan) is in attendance when men assemble for the worship of God. Though hidden from sight, he is working with all diligence to control the minds of the worshipers." (*The Great Controversy*, p. 518.)

Ellen White also described a meeting of Christians where the sound of vocal and instrumental music was heard with a frivolous song while the angels of God with sadness were moving away. (*Testimonies for the Church*, Vol. 1, p. 506.)

When the angels of God move away, could it then be possible that demons, cleverly and imperceptibly, mingle their secret demonic messages with the popular Christian songs performed?

An Australian pastor, Keith Piper, reports: "Christian Rock Albums are loaded with demonics." Piper lists several illustrations. For instance STRYPER's album In God we Trust, contains the hidden messages: "*Hail Lucifer – Satan who loves we worship.*" DANIEL BAND's album, Rise Up, has the hidden words: "*Now worship Satan – I shall love Satan – I am fighting back oh master demon.*" JERUSALEM's album, In His Majesty's Service, is backmasked with the words: "*Hey Lord Satan – Yarrh Satan he's master – Yarrh, Satan is Lord – Say I love you Satan – Jesus God He serves Satan – Oh we're yours Satan evil, oh evil, God is nil – My friend Lucifer sings for you.*"

Piper explains:

> It is very possible that the Rock rhythm and style is itself an invocation to demonic powers to participate... If demons are invoked through Rock then it is understandable that they will sing in duo with the artists, and as fans around the world listen and join in the songs, they form a planetary choir of satanic praise. (Answers, Chapter 82, http://www.users.on.net/mec/answers/.)

Godwin notes: "The demons just talk while their Rock and CCM dupes sing." (*What's Wrong with Christian Rock?* p. 144.) Referring to some music research examples, Godwin points out that there were "Demonic voices manifest in both forward and reverse modes during LIVE church worship. In one example, a demon voice like that of a young child rails against the preaching. Other manifestations praise Lucifer in reverse even as the church worship team sings normally."

Godwin concludes: "Once the doorway is opened, the demons say whatever they wish, regardless of the intent of the human voices." (Ibid., pp. 154, 155; Cf., Jan Voerman, *Secret Messages in the Church*, Geesbrug, Netherlands, 2008, pp. 13-18.)

Dan Lucarini, a musical leader of various churches, a former composer and rock specialist, writes:

> Can Satan's ploy work on Christians too? It can and it does. When we brought rock music (and all its musical cousins) into the church service, we invited along with it a spirit of immorality with which that music is unavoidably associated. It wasn't obvious at first. We didn't use hard rock; instead we used more acceptable, watered-down forms of it: soft rock, pop/rock, country rock and easy listening jazz styles...They were less edgy but still contained the underlying rock beat that undeniably appeals to our flesh and reminds us of the world's favourite music.

Dan continues:

> Despite all our efforts to restrain this musical beast, the saints of God are being seduced by CCM [Contemporary Christian Music] styles. These styles are capable of corrupting the morals of any Christian, no matter how strong they think they are...It all goes back to the big lie that 'God accepts me as I am; therefore he accepts my music'...
>
> Our acceptance of CCM into worship services has hurt an entire generation of older Christians, has led to church splits, and has created a breeding ground for immorality, selfishness and divisive attitudes in younger generations. These charges are a hard pill to swallow for any leader who has happily embraced CCM. No one knows this better than me.
>
> I had to admit that I too was deceived by my own lusts and selfishness. I was taken in by the big lie and its arguments, and the sinful spirits...hounded me. My devotion to CCM caused division in my marriage, confusion in my family and interfered with my personal relationship with Jesus. No matter how hard I tried, my music ministry did not seem to bear good fruit in people's lives by producing holiness and obedience...
>
> Contemporaries told me I was 'gifted by God' to lead praise and worship. I received strong affirmations of this from many pastors, denominational leaders, other musicians and the members of the congregations I served. How could one so 'gifted' fail? But I had

to flee from CCM's corrupting influence on my life...

Dan testifies:

> This is a very difficult book for me to write. I hate being wrong about anything I do for the Lord! All those hours spent working on music for him—were they wasted? I grieve when I let down my Lord and Saviour. I am hurt when I realize the effects on his church. But perhaps my experience can either prevent some from falling into or help others escape from the CCM trap. (Dan Lucarini, *Why I left the Contemporary Christian Music Movement,* Evangelical Press, 2003, pp. 42, 43, 46, 47.)

It is very true that "Debased music...destroys the rhythm of the soul and breaks down morality." We should, therefore, comply with the instruction:

> Great care should be exercised in the choice of music. Any melody partaking of the nature of jazz, rock, or related hybrid forms... will be shunned by persons of true culture. Let us use only good music in the home, in the social gathering, in the school, and in the church. (*SDA Church Manual,* 1990, p.146.)

Good music is characterized by its high aim:

> Music was made to serve a holy purpose, to lift the thoughts to that which is pure, noble, and elevating, and to awaken in the soul devotion and gratitude to God...Music forms a part of God's worship in the courts above, and we should endeavor, in our songs of praise, to approach as nearly as possible to the harmony of the heavenly choirs. (*Patriarchs and Prophets,* p. 594.)

It certainly will be profitable to note Mac Dominick's observation and follow his good advice:

> Music is usually **the first point of transition** in any congregation. It is **absolutely imperative** that pastors **resist** the pressure to use praise bands, contemporary 'rock' style praise choruses, terminate the use of the hymnal, and/or implementation of a 'contemporary service.' (*Outcome-Based Religion...*2005, p. 328. Emphasis added.)

Chapter 37

Temple-Service

We know that Israel enjoyed several musical instruments for daily occasions but it was commanded for the temple-services to make use of "cymbals, with psalteries, and with harps, according to the commandment of David, and of Gad the King's seer, and Nathan the prophet: for so was the commandment of the Lord by his prophets." (2 Chron. 29:25. Cf., 1 Chron. 25:6; 15:19–21.)

> Properly speaking, the real service of Praise in the Temple was only with the voice. This is often laid down as a principle by the rabbis. What instrumental music there was, served only to accompany and sustain the song...The melody was simple, sweet, and sung in unison to the accompaniment of instrumental music. Only one pair of brass cymbals were allowed to be used. But this 'sounding brass' and 'tinkling cymbal' formed no part of the Temple music itself, and served only as the signal to begin that part of the service...As already stated, the service of praise was mainly sustained by the human voice. (Alfred Edersheim, *The Temple, Its Ministry and Services,* pp. 76, 78, 80.)

> Musical sounds that dominate the solo voice and even the choir, as is the case very often in our days, would appear to the Eastern preposterous, and, according to their opinion, the aim of the musical performance would be missed if the words so much were brought to the background. (Moll, Veth, Domela Nieuwenhuis, *Bijbels Woordenboek*, p. 601.)

> Hebrew music was primarily vocal. The lyre was a common instrument used to accompany the human voice. (*Unger's Bible Dictionary*, p. 766.)

Nobody needs to be in doubt about the kinds of musical instruments the Lord required for sacred worship. Percussion instruments, like the drum, tambourine, timbrel, or tabret were mostly used by women at special occasions: a victory over the enemy, a joyful procession, a wedding, or other festivity. A percussion instrument,

> ...was generally played on festive occasions, but is never mentioned in connection with the services of the Temple...the Jews evidently had much variety in their instrumental music program. They were careful not to include certain instruments in divine services in the Temple, because they were not appropriate or conductive to worship. They used only those instruments which added dignity and beauty to their services. Others were reserved for the festive and secular occasions. (Paul McCommon, *Music in the Bible*, pp. 73, 74.)

The timbrel may have been excluded from the Temple instruments because of its great popularity with the Canaanite fertility cults. (*The Liberty Illustrated Bible Dictionary*, p. 736.)

Some instruments were considered 'unclean' and were not allowed in temple worship. (*Tyndale Bible Dictionary*, p. 923.)

In the OT the drum is used on festive occasions; it is not mentioned in connection with Divine service. (*The International Standard Bible Encyclopaedia*, vol. III, p. 2101.)

The timbrel, tambourine or tabret,

> was a typical women's instru`ment...Although it occurs in the Psalter and in religious hymns (Exod. 15; Jer. 31:4), it was not permitted in the temple. Its function in the Bible was restricted to secular or religious frolicking, cultic dances, or processions... (*The Interpreter's Dictionary of the Bible*, vol. 3, p. 474.)

Some argue that the use of rock music and the drum set in church is legitimized because cymbals were used in ancient worship. However, this ignores the fact that cymbals were not used to drive song rhythms, but merely to announce the beginning of a song or a stanza in the song. (Karl Tsatalbasidis, *Drums, Rock, and Worship*, p. 60.)

The cymbals in Bible times are not comparable to our drums; they were round, flat (copper) plates of only 10 to 15 cm in diameter and they made a nice and clear sound. (*Eerdmans Bible Encyclopedia*, p. 250.) The tambourine, tabret or timbrel, was normally a hand drum of small size used to beat the time and "they were only used at those religious feasts, which were combined with round dances and bore the character of a national festival." (Ed. Riehm, *Bijbels Woordenboek*, deel 2, p. 152.) These drums can hardly be compared with a modern drum set. Some of the Egyptian and Assyrian drums, however, seem to come a little closer to our modern drums and it seems plausible that the people of Israel used these kinds of drums at their idolatry services. (Cf. Fairbairn's *Imperial Standard Bible Encyclopedia*, vol. IV, p. 315.)

> Jingling, banging, and rattling accompanied heathen cults and the frenzying shawms of a dozen ecstatic rites intoxicated the masses…early synagogue song intentionally foregoes artistic perfection, renounces the playing of instruments, and attaches itself entirely to 'the word' – the text of the Bible…The use of instruments in the synagogue service was prohibited (and remained so, with certain exceptions), leaving music a strictly vocal art…Rabbis did not appreciate any kind of music that was merely pleasing to hear but had no edifying objective. It goes without saying that they condemned music that was likely to stir up excessive human passion…Song is regarded as a very desirable accompaniment to prayer. Musical performance at public worship was naturally subject to certain prohibitions…imitating rites of foreign worship... (*Encyclopaedia Judaica*, 1972, vol. 12, pp. 566, 598, 599.)

The writers who have most carefully investigated Jewish antiquities, and have written learnedly and elaborately in regard to the synagogue, concur in showing that its worship was destitute of instrumental music. (John L.Girardeau, *Instrumental Music in Church Worship*, p. 39.)

We read about music in Christian churches:

> Music in churches is as ancient as the Apostles, but instrumental music not so…Marinus Sanutus, who lived about the year 1290, was the first that brought the use of wind organs into churches, whence he was surnamed Torcellus, which is the name for an organ in the Italian tongue. (Bingham, *Origines Ecclesiasticae*, Bk. 8, ch. 7, Sect. 14.)

St. Mark's Organ

Some musical instruments and music styles are more at home in the concert hall than in the church.

Various sources clearly say that it wasn't allowed to use percussion instruments during the temple service. As in our days the drum can be associated with worldly music, so it was also the case in the days of the people of Israel. In dark days of unbelief and apostasy they worshiped strange gods and let their young children pass through the fire. "And they have built the high places of Tophet, which is in the valley of the son of Hinnom, to burn their sons and their daughters in the fire; which I commanded them not, neither came it into my heart." (Jer. 7:31. Cf. Jer. 19:5, 6. 2 Kings 23:10.)

The Hebrew word for drum is 'toph', while 'topheth' is derived from 'taphaph' which means: beating on a drum. In Strong's concordance you will find this also. There is a reference at 'topheth' (8611) to 'Taphaph' (8608).

Topheth was the place where idolatrous rituals took place in honour of Moloch and Baal. Parents came with their children who, at the climax of this gruesome worship, were sacrificed, by throwing them into the fire of the metal idol god during the sound of exciting music and the beat of drums.

The image of metal was made glowing hot by a fire kindled within it, and the children, laid in its arms, rolled from thence into the fiery lap below...even the first-born, nay the only child of the family, was given up. The parents stopped the cries of their children by fondling and kissing them, for the victim ought not to weep, and the sound of complaint was drowned in the din of flutes and kettle-drums. (Döllinger, *the Gentile and the Jew in the Courts of the Temple*...Vol. 1, p. 427.)

Tophet(h)...place...in the Hinnom Valley on the S.E. of Jerusalem,—where the royal gardens and 'music' ('Tophet' signifies 'tabret,' a type of all joyous music) pavilions of Solomon, through association with the rites performed in the adjoining idol-shrines... were succeeded by the abominations of the fire-idol's worship... (Haydn's Bible Dictionary, p. 626.)

Tophet...so called from the beating of drums to drown the cries of the children who were burned in the fire to Moloch. (John Brown, *A Dictionary of the Holy Bible*, p. 528.)

Topheth...From toph, the 'drums' beaten to drown the shrieks of the children made to pass through the fire to Moloch... (A. R. Fausset, *Bible Cyclopaedia*, p. 700.)

Tophet is supposed to have had its name from the drums which they beat, or the noises which they made, to drown the cries of their tortured children. (Scott, *Holy Bible*, Jer. 7:32.)

At the high place of Tophet (the word 'Tophet' has to do with the beating of a drum) the pagan priests carefully constructed stairways, altars and fire pits for the frenzied rites of Molech worship...As the drums pounded like enormous, overworked hearts ready to burst, musical instruments of all kinds were frantically blown and trumpeted to drown out the throat-shredding screams of dying children. Worshipers added their own howls to the chaos as they sang and wailed 'hymns' to the demons that were devouring their precious young...Rock & Roll is the modern equivalent of the Valley of Hinnom. The rock concert stage is today's 'High Place' of Tophet. The rock stars are the bug-eyed priests and our young people are the sacrificial babes...If God's people ever needed the discernment of the Holy Spirit, mixed with the righteous anger of the Almighty, that time is now. (Jeff Godwin, *Dancing with Demons,* pp. 9, 10.)

Chapter 38

Heavenly Music

According to the Bible, the greatest moment of all ages will be the coming of Christ, when all God's children are led into the house of the Father. What enormous joy and happiness will then be there. The victory is gained. There is once and for all an end to sin, misery, sickness, pain, fear and death. It will be an indescribable happening when God's children, with their beloved Redeemer, will be welcomed into God's kingdom. There are no words to describe this. It will surpass everything. "Eye hath not seen, nor ear heard, neither have entered into the heart of man, the things which God hath prepared for them that love Him." (1 Cor. 2:9.)

The entire universe vibrates with intense happiness. If there would ever be in the timeless eternity a memorable moment that may be celebrated with unknown lustre, then it surely is this all-surpassing moment. There is an overflow of gladness and thanksgiving with exuberant praise. Angels fly up and down with all kinds of musical instruments for an indescribable joyful service. Angels with golden drums are hovering close by, while other angels with huge bass guitars, decorated with sparkling diamonds, take their places around the throne of God. The tension increases as an ordering angel appears to give the signal that the delightful worship celebration service can begin and the overwhelming sounds of the mightiest praise service will be heard and the piercing music, and exciting drum beat fills the universe...

Can you imagine exciting drum beat filling the universe? Will it ever be like that in heaven? Is that really what will happen? Will it be indeed something like a "sanctified" heavenly rock-concert? Can you really believe that?

What does the Bible tell us?

"The four beasts and the four and twenty elders fell down before the Lamb having every one of them harps... and they sung a new song..." (Rev. 5:8, 9.) The 144,000 redeemed sung a new song before the throne of God: "And I heard the voice of harpers harping with their harps." (Rev. 14:2.) And those who gained the victory "stand on the sea of glass, having the harps of God. They sing the song of Moses... and the song of the Lamb." (Rev. 15:2, 3.)

We don't read that there will be a holy rock concert in God's kingdom with drums and bass-guitars. No, nothing of that kind! Only the instrument that God prescribed by David and the prophets to play in the temple and to accompany the sacred psalms. In God's eternal kingdom the sound of the harp will accompany the songs of God's redeemed children.

> Before entering the City of God, the Saviour bestows upon His followers the emblems of victory and invests them with the insignia of their royal state... For each there is a crown, bearing his own 'new name'...and the inscription, 'Holiness to the Lord.' In every hand are placed the victor's palm and shining harp. Then, as the commanding angels strike the note, every hand sweeps the harp strings with skillful touch, awaking sweet music in rich, melodious strains. Rapture unutterable thrills every heart, and each voice is raised in grateful praise... Amid the waving of palm branches they pour forth a song of praise, clear, sweet, and harmonious; every voice takes up the strain, until the anthem swells through the vaults of heaven: 'Salvation to our God which sitteth upon the throne, and unto the Lamb.' And all the inhabitants of heaven respond in the ascription: 'Amen: Blessing, and glory, and wisdom, and thanksgiving, and honor, and power, and might, be unto our God for ever and ever.' (E. G. White, *The Great Controversy,* pp. 645, 646, 650.)

> There will be music there, and song, such music and song as, save in the visions of God, no mortal ear has heard or mind conceived... I have been shown the order, the perfect order, of heaven, and have been enraptured as I listened to the perfect music there. After coming out of vision, the singing here has sounded very harsh and discordant... There is one angel who always leads, who first touches the harp and strikes the note, then all join in the rich, perfect music of

heaven. It cannot be described. It is melody, heavenly, divine, while from every countenance beams the image of Jesus, shining with glory unspeakable... What a song that will be when the ransomed of the Lord meet...! All heaven is filled with rich music, and with songs of praise to the Lamb. (E. G. White, *Maranatha*, p. 361.)

> There is no 'neutral' music... There is music that is to serve God—to glorify God—inspired and sustained by God's Spirit; and there is music in serving satan that is controlled and specified by the spirit of this world. (R. Ebertshäuser, *Der Charismatische 'Lobpreis': Fremdes Feuer im Heiligtum Gottes*, s. 5.)

Our rebellious world is soon going to perish. Are we following God's Word and do we obey His commandments? Are we keeping the faith of Jesus or do we want to follow the modern church-growth movement and soon be a part of the apostate New Age world-church? Do we praise God with devoted music or do we dishonour Him with worldly, popular Christian music and songs? Do we heed the God-given warnings? Are we willing to testify of the heavenly message that has been given us?

The world is waiting for our dedicated effort. There has never been such an intense interest for the word of prophecy. Worldwide admiration for prophetic themes is at the highest point of all times. (*Amazing Facts*, Jan. 2005.)

Although God's children are not popular in this world and will face great problems, God promises His faithful followers help and protection.

> In the closing period of earth's history the Lord will work mightily in behalf of those who stand steadfastly for the right... Satan with all the hosts of evil cannot destroy the weakest of God's saints. Angels that excel in strength will protect them, and in their behalf Jehovah will reveal Himself as a 'God of gods,' able to save to the uttermost those who have put their trust in Him. (E. G. White, *Maranatha*, p. 270.)

> To him that overcometh will I grant to sit with me in my throne, even as I also overcame, and am set down with my Father in his throne. (Rev. 3:21.)

Appendix I

Crosslinked Influences

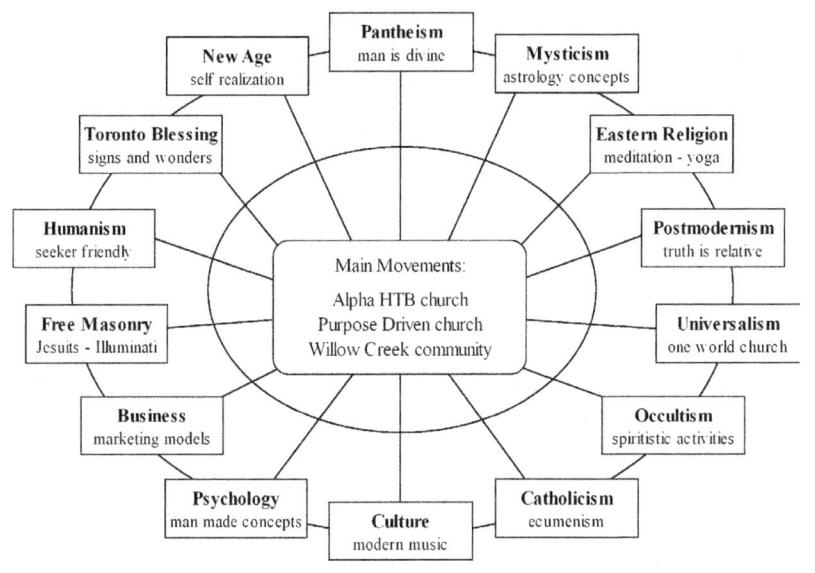

Main Movements:
Alpha HTB church
Purpose Driven church
Willow Creek community

Surrounding influences:
- **New Age** — self realization
- **Pantheism** — man is divine
- **Mysticism** — astrology concepts
- **Toronto Blessing** — signs and wonders
- **Eastern Religion** — meditation - yoga
- **Humanism** — seeker friendly
- **Postmodernism** — truth is relative
- **Free Masonry** — Jesuits - Illuminati
- **Universalism** — one world church
- **Business** — marketing models
- **Occultism** — spiritistic activities
- **Psychology** — man made concepts
- **Culture** — modern music
- **Catholicism** — ecumenism

Some prominent crosslinked worldly influences that shaped and/or reflect the modern church growth movement.

The modern church-growth movement has adapted ancient heathen religious profiles as well as current scientific techniques and insights. There is no doubt as to the driving force behind these influences and the degrading effect upon the churches of present-day Christianity.

Meditation in particular unites Eastern religion with Western Christianity. The church-growth leaders advocate disciplines similar to Zen, Mantra and Kundalini such as Contemplative- Centering- and Breath prayers, Lectio Divina, Entering the Silence and Creative Visualization techniques by which the imaginary desired results are realised and contact is made with higher powers. Thus "Contemplative Spirituality" also known as the "Spiritual Formation Movement" smoothly paves the way for the working of evil spirits within the church and in people's lives. The spirits "will profess faith" and "respect" church-institutions *"and their work will be accepted as a manifestation of divine power."* (*The Great Controversy,* p. 588.)

Rick Warren, referring to this "Spiritual Formation Movement" as well as to other modern trends stresses the importance of their "valid message for the church" as "a wake up call" each emphasizing "a different purpose of the church." (*The Purpose Driven Church,* p. 127.) This much promoted movement of personal spiritual disciplines will result in a mystic religious unity of universal apostasy and prepare the world for the final battle between good and evil. Ellen White cautions:

> Little by little he (Satan) has prepared the way for his masterpiece of deception in the development of spiritualism...the whole world will be swept into the ranks of this delusion. The people are vast being lulled to a fatal security, to be awakened only by the outpouring of the wrath of God. (The Great Controversy, pp. 561, 562.)

Appendix II
Toronto & Kundalini

Some comparisons between the experiences of the Toronto Movement and the Occultic Eastern Kundalini Yoga.

	Toronto Blessing	**Kundalini**
PURPOSES		
	Healing	Healing
	Spiritual progress	Spiritual progress
	Experience love & peace	Experience bliss
	Deliverance	Liberation
TRIGGERS		
	Spontaneous-no warning	Spontaneous
	Repetitive music	Repetitive music
	Letting control of mind go	Wandering mind
	Feeling of despair	Feeling of despair
PHYSICAL SIGNS		
Body	Body curls (pre-natal)	Bends forward or back
	Trembling	Trembling
	Numbness in parts	Partial parlysis
Mouth	Clenched jaws	Clenched jaws
	Increase saliva	Increase saliva
Eyes	Rolled back	Rolled back
	Twitching/moving	Rotating
	Can't open eyes	Can't open eyes
Face	Wrinkles up	Wrinkles up

	Brows knit	Brows knit
Breathing	Constricted breathing Breathing patterns change	Constricted breathing Breathing patterns change
Actions	Rolling on floor Body twists Body raises up and down Crawling on floor Patterned movements	Rolling on floor Body twists Body raises up and down Creeping Hands move in patterns
Voice	Unable to speak Speaking in tongues Unusual sounds (animal)	Loss of speech Speaking in tongues Unusual sounds (animal)

INTERNAL

Sensations	Heat Energy flow in body Tingling Pressed to floor Head to feet sensations Orgasms	Heat Energy flows Tingling Pressed to floor Head to feet sensations Sexual excitement
Visions	Lights Visions of angels	Lights Visions of dieties
Mental	Phenomena passed on Awareness of being Christ Periods of in-activity Revelations	Absorbing of symptoms New Awareness Period of in-activity Existential insights
Emotional	Giddy Laughing Crying Emotional releases Restlessness	Giddy Laughing Crying Emotional releases Restlessness

REASON FOR EXPERIENCE VARIATION		
	Amount of change needed	Amount of balance
	Expected results	Conditioning
	Past history	Past history
SYMPTOMS		
	Linger for months	Linger for months

(Also a feeling of anger can be experienced in the Toronto Blessing and in Kundalini Yoga.)

Sources on Toronto:

Christian History, Issues 23, 45.
Mainstream, Summer 1994.
SCP Newsletter, Fall 1994.
Media Spotlight, Special Report, 1995.
Personal observations & interviews.

Sources on Kundalini:

Mookerjee, Ajit, "Kundalini: The Arousal of the Inner Energy," *Destiny*, 1991.

Interviews.

(DesVoignes, Greg, *Holy Laughter & Company, A Toronto Blessing...Or Kundalini Curse?* Christian Research Ministries, Spokane, WA 99208 USA.)

Appendix III

God's Church & The Paradigm Church

Some fundamental differences beween God's true church and the New Paradigm Church.

God's True Church	New Paradigm Church
Identify with Divine Standards and apply them in all church activities.	Identify with local culture and adjust all services and programs accordingly.
Use a distinct name for the church.	A neutral name should be chosen.
Preach the Word of God.	Preach a seeker-sensitive message.
The Spirit and the power of the two-edged sword should convince people of sin and bring about repentance; unite and enable them to live by faith a new-born sanctified life in Christ Jesus unto eternal salvation.	Technology, psychology and marketing techniques with visualization and dramatic presentations are to be utilized to attract, unite and hold people together to practise a certain religious standard of living.
Use a reliable Bible translation as close as possible to the original pure text such as the Byzantine Text and Textus Receptus.	Use preferably paraphrased versions as close as possible to the people but mainly based on less reliable Alexandrian texts.
Follow the Biblical instructions how to reach people with the Gospel of salvation.	Employ marketing research to identify the needs and desires of the people.
Reprove, rebuke and exhort.	Entertain, satisfy and appease.
Aim at people's true conversion.	Promote a sense of feeling good.
Crucify self.	Cultivate self-esteem.
Stress the importance of growing in grace.	Stress the importance of great numbers.

God's True Church	New Paradigm Church
A foundation of sound biblical doctrine is the basis for people's spiritual life.	People's spiritual life is guided by Eastern practices of contemplative spirituality.
Doctrinal purity forms the ground for true unity and freedom.	Unity is stressed at the expense of sound doctrine.
Biblical truth must be proclaimed, upheld, guarded and defended.	Life applicated messages of man's needs must be more stressed than divine truth.
The objective of worship is to serve God.	The motive for worship is to like people.
The church is separated from the world.	The church is embracing the world.
Music is to praise God sacredly.	Music is to please and attract people.
The influence of music is not neutral nor amoral. Popular music is not purified by religious lyrics. Only edifying hymns and music styles that honour God and are a blessing to man are to be accepted.	All kinds of music are acceptable. There is no Christian music; only Christian lyrics. Contemporary modern music styles and songs people are accustomed to listen to should be used to revive worship services.
The church choir should evoke a holy and dedicated atmosphere.	A modern praise band is to excite and capture people's emotional feelings.
The church is to unite faithful believers in Christ as their personal Saviour.	The church should unite all religions into one world church with Christ as one way.
Values man's conscience and suffers even those who may be regarded as tares. They are left to grow up until the harvest.	Shows intolerance towards conservatives seeking to get rid of all those who disagree and are not co-operative.
Avoids political inroads and any mingling of church and state confessing that God's Kingdom is not of this world.	Incorporates politics and the economical world encouraging collaboration with state-governments.
Taking heed of the sure word of prophecy explaining its meaning is a necessary part of our mission against deception.	Discourages the study of the prophetic word emphasizing our mission as being our business.

Appendix IV

BREAKING NEWS ?

A closer look at Willow Creek's failure.
Willow Creek repents. A public confession:
"We made a mistake."

In October 2007, Bill Hybels, pastor of the influential Willow Creek Community Church in America, admitted: "We made a mistake."

This recognition, made after 30 years of doing church on the basis of worldly, psychological and commercial principles, is significant.

The Willow Creek way of doing church is illustrated by James Twitchell, who reports in his book, *Shopping for God*, that outside the office of Pastor Hybels hangs a poster stating: "What is our business? Who is our customer? What does the customer consider value?" (*Christianity Today*, October 2007)

It is clear that Willow Creek's leading pastor in the ministry of his 'spiritual' congregation is driven by secular business slogans.

After a special in-depth study about the effectiveness of Willow Creek's ministry, the result is shocking. Hybels himself calls it "earth shaking - ground breaking and mind blowing."

During the *Leadership Summit Conference* he admitted:

> Some of the stuff that we have put millions of dollars into thinking it would really help our people grow and develop spiritually, when the data actually came back it wasn't helping people that much.

So millions of dollars were spent in thinking that the Willow Creek approach to ministry would help people spiritually but in truth it was of no real help. Thus the predictions made by many over the years, including, for example, G. A. Pritchard in his evaluation of 1996, has proven to be all too true. The shocking thing is that in general there is no real spiritual quality present in the Willow Creek community.

The results of the investigation, published in the book *Reveal: Where are you?* makes clear that spiritual growth does not come through an interesting seekers' friendly, worldly-orientated ministry but by age-old spiritual methods and practices that are in harmony with the Bible. Thus, in order to aim at real spiritual growth, the *old paths* should be asked for and that will not require multi-million dollar facilities or hundreds of staff to manage.

Willow Creek made a serious mistake. It thought that people would be helped spiritually but in reality it was an idle illusion. Greg Hawkins, executive pastor of Willow Creek and co-author of the book *Reveal: Where are you?* explains that they now have a dream to change their ministry fundamentally:

> Our dream is that we fundamentally change the way we do church. That we take out a clean sheet of paper and we rethink all of our old assumptions. Replace it with new insights. Insights that are informed by research and rooted in Scripture. Our dream is really to discover what God is doing and how he's asking us to transform this planet.

The sad thing is, however, that many churches around the world followed, more or less, in Willow Creek's footsteps. And now it has turned out that this mega-church movement did not administer proper methods to preach effectively a correct biblical message.

Is Willow Creek's confession after doing church for more than 30 years a surprising revelation? The answer should be a clear No! After 13 years of doing church there were many serious and penetrating questions about the biblical design and effectiveness of Willow Creek's seeker-friendly approach.

Bill Hybels, as founder and pastor of the Willow Creek Church, was confronted early in his ministry with the fact that many "conversions" did not last long. Hybels admitted then that this was terribly painful for him. He testified:

The honest answers were terribly painful for me to admit. Over the course of thirteen years in this church, thousands of people have proven to be rocky-soiled people, thorny-soiled people whose faith has faded. (G. A. Pritchard, *Willow Creek Seeker Services, Evaluating a New Way of Doing Church*, p. 277.)

Pritchard, who studied Willow Creek for his doctoral dissertation, reports that one staff member even argued that many individuals, who have been baptized and around the church for years, were not even believers. Another staff member said that this tendency at Willow Creek produced "numbers but not disciples." (Ibid., pp. 277, 278.)

Thus, it is not surprising that many Willow Creek members, not being true disciples, slip away. Pritchard reports that a pastor from the area, described "how many committed Creekers regularly end up joining his more traditional, Bible-teaching church after years of running on the Willow Creek treadmill." (Ibid., p. 284.)

Willow Creek's characterizing phenomenon is explained in these words:

A constant stream of individuals is attracted through Willow Creek's front door to the excitement of their program. But many of these same participants eventually feel the overwhelming pressure of its dualistic theology and slip out the back door. (Ibid.)

Pritchard observed a number of faults and deficiencies in Willow Creek's ministry, noting:

…there is a lack of emphasis on Christian truth… Willow Creek does not teach substantial biblical truth consistently on the weekend. (Ibid., p. 276.)

Willow Creek's weekend messages combine the marketing emphasis on satisfying felt needs with the psychological ethics of seeking fulfilment. (Ibid., p. 251.)

The holiness of God and the convicting nature of God's moral law are obscured… Hybels did not teach about God's moral law or warn his listeners to examine themselves to see if they were truly in the faith… Weekend listeners are rarely confronted with God's moral law or challenged strongly to grow in their understanding. (Ibid., pp. 263, 264, 286.)

When a church-wide survey was made about participation in sins such as lying, stealing, adultery and viewing pornography, Hybels broke the news that large percentages of the congregation had participated in these sins. However, he did not rebuke the congregation, but rather complimented them. When a week later Hybels noted that a large percentage "admitted having illicit sexual relationships," again, Hybels did not call for repentance but instead emphasized God's compassionate love. (Ibid., p. 264.)

Pritchard also affirms that Hybels realized that his messages and ministry were a dilution of the gospel:

> In 1979, Hybels repented from this watery gospel and began to teach about the holiness of God… 'He said the Lord had been convicting him about his sermons. He said from now on he would be preaching straight from the Bible, that it was the only honest thing he could do before God… (Ibid., p. 239.)

Unfortunately, this commendable attitude did not last very long. Pritchard continues: "However, the use of psychology in his messages quickly returned." (Ibid.)

Almost ten years later, another confession was made. Pritchard reports:

> Hybels has admitted this need to make the gospel clearer. After his 1988 study break, Hybels confessed to his staff, 'We've been too helpful to people.' (Ibid., p. 278.)

However, in spite of this further confession, Pritchard explains: "During my analysis of the weekend messages, I discovered Hybels repeatedly returning to three academic disciplines: psychology, apologetics, and business management." (Ibid.) No wonder that the preaching of a distorted gospel does not produce genuinely converted, born-again people. Pritchard, touching this fundamental deficiency, tells:

> Another staff member admitted that many church attenders have never made 'a very humble cry for God's mercy, founded on the faith that Christ died for our sins and then asking or pleading and

trusting for him to come in and change my heart such that I can be presented before him as a regenerate person.' (Ibid., p. 278.)

It is indeed a very painful thought for the Willow Creek leaders that their ministry has been biblically ineffective. The true essence of the gospel is lacking. There has been no real conversion and no true discipleship.

The fundamental commission of Jesus: *'Go ye therefore, and make disciples of all nations'* (Matt. 28:19, KJV margin), will not be truly fulfilled when a worldly approach with psychological aspects and business principles is exercised. Such a ministry must be viewed as found wanting. Willow Creek's marketing perspective has turned out to be a subtle and deadly shift in Christianity.

Furthermore it is a legitimate question to ask why this unbiblical approach was continued while, during the early years of doing church, it was more than once clearly revealed and admitted that good results were not forthcoming. It took another seventeen years for another drastic and similar confession to be made.

How many churches around the world followed Willow Creeks' faulty approach? Someone, who visited Willow Creek faithfully for a period of twenty years, who still loves the Willow Creek people and appreciates their zeal, may, with his testimony, perhaps be a voice for all those who did not find spiritual rest in Willow Creek's mega church:

> "But, looking back and today I believe Willow Creek is a 'Para church' instead of an actual Biblical Church and should be called so due to the lack of discipleship that I now know I experienced and know so many others have experienced."

During the years this former Creeker has met many people who were disillusioned and spiritually hurt. He points out that there is a lack of fearing God:

> "Going forward I believe the leadership needs to focus more on fearing what God thinks instead of fearing what man thinks. I believe there should be a formal apology. I've been hurt; many people have been hurt."

He points to two clear Bible texts: Gal. 1:10 about seeking to please men or God and 2 Tim. 4:3 predicting that the time will come where sound teaching will not be endured and teachers will be chosen that have itching ears.

(Posted by: Former Creeker at October 26, 2007; http://blog.christianitytoday.com/outofur/archives/2007/10/willow_creek_re_1.html)

Will Willow Creek with its philosophical and commercial perspectives ever become a pure biblical church? Are the various churches worldwide that followed Willow Creek's principles thoroughly shaken up now? Will they now pay undivided attention to the principles of God's Word instead of following blindly unbiblical mega church methods? Only time will reveal the answers to these questions.

We invite you to view the complete
selection of titles we publish at:

www.TEACHServices.com

or write or email us your praises,
reactions, or thoughts about this
or any other book we publish at:

TEACH Services, Inc.
P.O. Box 954
Ringgold, GA 30736

info@TEACHServices.com

Finally, if you are interested in seeing
your own book in print, please contact us at

publishing@teachservices.com.

We would be happy to review your manuscript for free.